discovering
Barcelona

a travel guide for teens

"What strange phenomena we find in a great city
like Barcelona, all we need do is stroll about with our
eyes open. Life swarms with innocent monsters"

based on a free adaptation of a quote by poet Charles Baudelaire

All the information in this guide is subject to change.
I recommend that you call ahead –or check the relevant
website– to obtain current information before traveling.

Publishing information

Discovering Barcelona, a travel guide for teens
ISBN-13: 978-84-616-5745-2 ● ISBN-10: 84-616-5745-4

Enric Massó
Apt. de Correus 9103 ● 08080 BARCELONA, Catalonia (Spain, EU)
www.discoveringbarcelona.info || www.bit.ly/discoveringbarcelona
Cover Image: © flickr/ Kevin Krejci. Thank you Kai!

For bulk order prices or any other inquiries, please contact: enric@discoveringbarcelona.info

Errata, Corrections & Updates: **www.discoveringbarcelona.info**

discovering
Barcelona
a travel guide for teens

by Enric Massó
pronounced "an-rick mah-soh"

This book does not aim to be a typical tourist guide covering only monuments, museums and other very interesting but often boring facts about the place you're visiting. Instead, this is a "guide for teens" to attractions and activities that I am sure you'll enjoy more while in Barcelona. Let's show adults that they can also see many of those things while you're having fun along the way.

Understanding the navigation

I have divided the city in five zones so it's easier for you to locate the places and activities without having to learn a bunch of district and neighbourhood names.

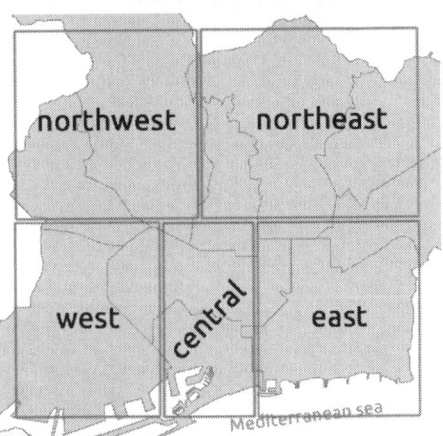

Plan your visit

Find here all what you need to know: addresses, websites, phone numbers and opening hours, plus...

HOW MUCH DOES IT COST?

TRAM   METRO   BUS   TRAIN

 THEY'VE GOT A CAFE

 SOUVENIR SHOP

 GOOD FOR A RAINY DAY

 AGE/HEIGHT RESTRICTIONS

... and **Lat.** and **Long.** indicating the coordinates to get there... if you have a GPS smartphone!

Betcha didn't know
Discover fascinating facts related to the attraction you're visiting.

My advice

A section for travel tips and insider advice. This bit is to let you know stuff related to the activity I think you might be interested in. Show off by letting everybody else know that you know!

Photo Ops

Something you shouldn't miss, such as hanging from the tusks of the stone mammoth in the Parc de la Ciutadella. Get your camera ready!

The Best...

There is also a chapter with **The Best** lists telling you important information like where to find superb restaurants, and awesome shops. Oh, and you'll also find maps at the start of each section to help you to work out which places are close to each other.

Pronouncing places

I have included the pronunciation of the different places for you to learn how to speak like a local. Note that the underscore indicates where you should emphasize your pronunciation.

Where is **Barcelona?**

(pronounced "bar-sah-lo-nah", and please, no twisting your tongue with the 'c')

Barcelona

THE BIG BIG EUROPE

welcome!

Can you find Barcelona in a map of Europe? Look for the Iberian Peninsula, down to the left, where Spain and Portugal are located. Then zoom into the coast facing the Mediterranean Sea and move a bit upwards towards the Pyrenees, just there you'll see a triangle shaped region called **Catalonia**. At half way, on the coast, you will see Barcelona, its capital city. It does not look like much, does it? Compare it to the size of England, France or Germany. Yet this 32 thousand-square-kilometres area -roughly the size of the state of Maryland in the US- is the birthplace of famous artists like Gaudí or Miró; home to great football players like Cesc, Puyol, Xavi, Iniesta, Neymar and Messi; set for popular singers like Serrat, Gisel·la, Dyango or Llach; headquarters to influential organisations, companies and universities and an important economic region in Europe. It is full of history, famous buildings, art masterpieces, some of the best summer resorts in the Mediterranean and delicious cuisine... and it packs 7.5 million people, 65% of which live in the metropolitan area of Barcelona! •

Contents

ATTRACTIONS & ACTIVITIES

Discover fun things you can do while visiting Barcelona

17

Check page 220 for a list in alphabetical order

ROUTE PLANNER

Where to go and what to do the easy way, the lazy way!

153

THE BEST...

Places to have a treat and must-see shops

173

20 things I love to do in BARCELONA

204

SHOPPING TIME!

Locate the shopping areas in Barcelona where you'll find all the major brands. **181**

DISCOVERYHUNT

Visiting the Old City district while on an exciting fact discovery hunt.

188

v.1.0/1307

Hola!

An adventure is waiting for you

Ready for an adventure? You've come to the right place! There's a lot to see and do in Barcelona. This guide will help you to get the most out of your experience. To make the most out of your trip, before you leave, read the section "*A bit of background and some fun facts*" where you'll get a glimpse of Barcelona's main facts, history and culture.

Maps, there are plenty of those. You should familiarise yourself with the location of the main monuments and attractions so you can better assist your parents when they get lost... and they eventually will, trust me!

Also, look at the addresses and websites in the "*Attractions & Activities*" section. Nearly all websites will pop up in one of the local languages but don't worry, just look for the word 'Welcome', 'English', 'ENG' or 'EN' and click over it. Now the page is in English... magic! For some attractions you have to line up early in the morning, especially during the busy summer months. These web addresses will also help you research details such as handicap accessibility, admission fees and seasonal changes in hours.

To make things easy, I have proposed some routes that you can follow. This will save you some planning time and you will be able to focus on enjoying the trip. Very important: I have also included sections to tell you the best places to eat, shop, play... don't miss it!

Now for the fun part: the "*Discovery Hunt*". A challenging adventure where you will have to unravel clues in each step of the hunt that will ultimately reveal to you a secret place. But if you get stuck, don't worry, you have the solutions at the end of the guide. No peeping!

Other sections that will help you are the "*Useful tips*" and the things I think it's good to know about Barcelona, like customs, schedules, weather, etc. I know you are on vacation, but take the opportunity to practice some foreign language. Check some short sentences in Catalan –the local language– which I've prepared for you so you can communicate with the locals. And I am also sharing the 20 things I like to do in Barcelona. Hope you like them.

In the very back there is an index, where you can look up the page numbers for specific attractions or activities you want to read about. Enjoy your stay in my hometown and let me know what you liked the most (and the least too!) •

Things to do, places to see

Are you ready to visit Barcelona? Read this guide before you leave, then carry it with you while you're there. It will help you to choose what you want to do each day. Initial planning for a trip is time for dreaming. I will paint you a picture of Barcelona and you can imagine yourself in it.

Instead of providing an endless list of neighbourhoods, historical sites, museums and other boring landmarks, I have organised this guide around 60+ *"Attractions and Activities"* which I have handpicked myself especially for you. Mark those that you want to visit by ticking the box on the top right hand side of the page of each activity. Not sure where to start?.... check the 'Index by Type' on page 222.

Gettin' your bearings...

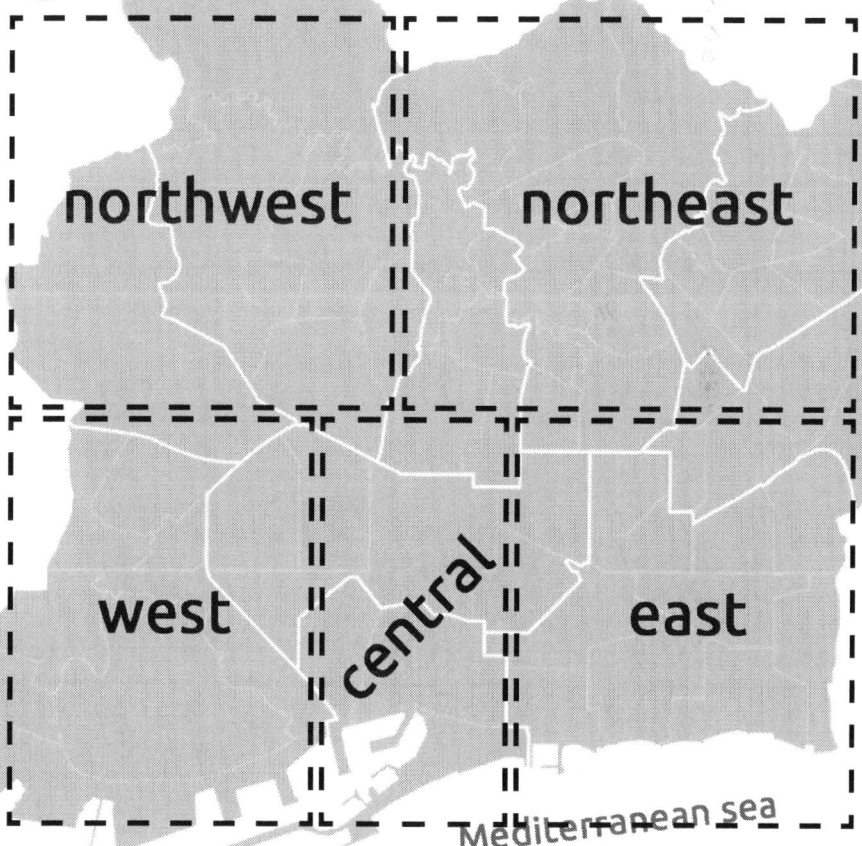

northwest

northeast

west

central

east

Mediterranean sea

THE CITY OF BARCELONA

A bit of history...

Barcelona has emerged from a spotty history. With Castilian kings pumping cannonballs over the city walls and anarchists disagreeing on which shoulder to hang their rifles, the city shrank in the shadow of greater cities and powers for centuries.

Though founded around 230 BC, likely by the Carthaginians, and invaded by the Visigoths and then briefly by the Muslims, the history of the city, in a sense, only truly began after armies from what is now France pushed back the Muslims in 801 AD. At the time, the plains and mountains to the northwest and north of Barcelona were populated by the people who by then could be identified as 'Catalans' (although surviving documentary references to the term only date to the 10th century). 'Catalans' are the inhabitants of Catalonia and 'Catalan' is their language. Catalan language derives from Latin.

Between 1040 and 1075, Count Ramon Berenguer I weaved a dense network of alliances among the noble and rich in Catalonia and abroad and gradually established the House of Barcelona as the ruling power in the country, becoming the de-facto capital since.

In the 12th century, Catalonia grew rich on pickings from the fall of the Muslim caliphate of Cordoba. The Catalans managed to keep their creative forces alight through to the 14th century, when Barcelona ruled an empire including Sicily, Malta, Sardinia, Valencia, the Balearics, the French regions of Rousillon and Cerdagne and parts of Greece. But by the 15th century, devastated by the plague, spectacular bank crashes, and the Genoese squeezing their markets, the empire ran out of steam. While the Catalans may have hoped that union with the kingdom of Castile would pump cash back into the coffers and vitality onto the streets, heirs to the crown of Castile were more interested in juicing Catalonia to finance their own imperial ambitions.

A 1462 rebellion against King Joan II ended in a siege in 1473 that devastated the city. Barcelona was more or less annexed into the Castilian state into what later became Spain, but was excluded from the plundering of the Americas that brought fantastic riches to 16th century Castile. By now, the peasants had started to revolt. Disaffected Catalans resorted to arms a number of times, and the last revolt, during the War of the Spanish Succession, saw Catalonia siding with Britain and Austria against Philip V, the French contender for the Spanish throne. That was their undoing. Barcelona fell in Sep 11th, 1714 after another shocking siege, and as well as banning the Catalan language, Philip built a huge fort, the Ciutadella, to watch over his ungrateful subjects in town.

After 1778 Catalonia was permitted to trade with America, and the region's fortunes gradually turned around. Spain's first industrial revolution, based on cotton, was launched here, and other industries based on wine, cork and iron also developed. By the 1830s, the European Romantic movement virtually rescued Catalan culture and language just as it was in danger of disappearing. The Catalan Renaixença, or Renaissance, was a crusade led by poets and writers to popularise the people's language. A fervent nationalist movement sprang up around the same time, and was embraced by all parties of the political spectrum.

The decades around the turn of the century were a fast ride, with anarchists, Republicans, bourgeois regionalists, gangsters, police

PLAÇA DEL REI, THE CENTRE OF CATALAN POWER DURING THE MIDDLE AGES

terrorists, political gunmen and centrists in Madrid all clamouring for a slice of the action. This followed an explosion in Barcelona's population from around 115,000 in 1800 to more than half a million by 1900, then over a million by 1930 as workers flocked in for industrial jobs. As many as 80% of the city's workers embraced the anarchist CNT by the end of WWI, and industrial relations hit an all time low during a wave of strikes in 1919-20 when employers hired assassins to kill union leaders.

Within days of Spain's Second Republic forming in 1931, Catalan nationalists declared an independent republic within an 'Iberian Federation' but Madrid intervened again to quash this desire. Catalonia briefly gained genuine autonomy after the leftist Popular Front won the February 1936 Spanish general election, and for nearly a year revolutionary anarchists and the Workers Marxist Unification Party ran the town. In July 1936, part of the Spanish army -led by rebel General Franco- revolted against the democratically elected Republic and the Spanish Civil War started.

Get 10 anarchists in a room, though, and you'll have 11 political opinions; in May 1937 infighting between communists and anarchists broke out into street fighting for three days, killing at least 1,500 people. The Republican effort across Spain was troubled by similar infighting, which destroyed any chance they may have had of defeating Franco's fascist militia. Barcelona, the last

major stronghold of the Republicans, fell to Franco's forces in January 1939, and the war ended a few months later. Rather than submitting to Franco, thousands of Catalans fled across the border to France, Andorra and farther afield.

Franco wasted no time in instating a dictatorship in Spain disbanding along the way Catalan institutions and banning Catalan language in the process, and flooding the region with impoverished immigrants from Andalucía in the vain hope that the pesky Catalans, with their continual movements for independence, would be swamped. But the plan soured somewhat when the migrants' children and grandchildren turned out to be more Catalan than the Catalans. Franco even banned one of the Catalans' joyful expressions of national unity, the sardana, a public circle dance.

But they'd barely turned the last sods on the dictator's grave in 1975 when Catalonia burst out again in an effort to recreate itself again as a great nation. Catalan was revived with a vengeance, the Generalitat, or local government, was reinstated, and today, people gather all over town several times a week to dance the sardana. While there's still talk of independence, it remains just that... talk (for now!). Barcelona is its country's most happening town, and seems set to stay that way •

fun facts
about Barcelona

...is 101.4 km² -39.2 sq miles- and is divided in 10 districts, 75 neighbourhoods and is home to 1.7 million inhabitants and a total of nearly 5 million in the whole metropolitan area, which comprises 36 cities and towns, including Barcelona.

...is to thank for World Book Day, **La Diada de Sant Jordi** (Saint George's Day) is a national feast day in the region and on this day it is a tradition to present your near and dear ones with roses and books. This was the inspiration for the UNESCO to declare April 23rd as the International Day of Books.

...is considered the "*best beach city*" in the world by National Geographic with more than 4.5km of coastline, but their beaches weren't massively used for leisure until the Olympic Games of 1992.

...has a large portion of the city devoted exclusively to pedestrians, a total of 130 hectares equivalent to 260 football fields. So if you are in Barcelona you might want to start loving to walk!

... has the most walked down street in Spain, the **Portal de l'Àngel**, a busy shopping street. Walk down there and you will be one among approximately 3,500 others who throng the street every hour!

...you won't find many 'flamenco' shows in town. Even though Spain is well known for its flamenco dancing, this popular dance is not traditional in Barcelona or Catalonia. Catalans prefer the more contemporary rock'n'roll scene. They're not fond of 'toreros' either. In fact, bull fighting was banned in the region in 2010.

Our symbols

FLAG OF CATALONIA

You were told you were going to spend a few vacation days in Spain, so you might have expected to find the Spanish flag (3 stripes, red-yellow-red) flying everywhere, didn't you? But then you haven't... what's going on? Well, you have arrived in Barcelona, the capital of Catalonia and, while still being part of Spain, we Catalans have our own flag which is a bit different. It's called **la Senyera** and it consists of 4 red stripes on a golden background, which, in practice is like having 9 stripes -4 red and 5 yellow- but still a bit short of the American flag, which contains 13.

You are going to find both flags -the Catalan and the Spanish one- waving at government buildings, hotels and police stations but in most other occasions you will find the Catalan flag flying on its own -or alongside the EU flag.

The Senyera (meaning 'pennon', 'banner', 'ensign', or, more generically, 'flag' in Catalan) is the flag of Catalonia and one of the oldest flags in Europe to be used in the present day, but not in continuous use since its creation. It is believed the first appearance of the flag is on a seal in the 12th century, although its mythological origin is also linked to Wilfred the Hairy when, after a battle, Frank King Charles the Bald wiped his fingers in the blood of the nobleman and drew four red bars on his golden shield as an emblem. The senyera pattern is also nowadays in the flag of different territories of the former Crown of Aragon.

The shield of the city of Barcelona is a combination of the cross of St. George, patron saint of the House of Barcelona and the flag of the Counts of Barcelona. The royal arms (four vertical red bars on a gold field) gave rise to the shield of the Crown of Aragon (as of 1137, date of the wedding of Count Ramon Berenguer IV and Petronila, daughter of the Aragonese king Ramiro II). King Peter III granted the royal arms to the city on July 4, 1345 and the cross as a distinctive sign of the city, is already found on a stamp in 1288 ●

SHIELD OF THE CITY OF BARCELONA

The *Estelada* or 'starred flag' or 'lone star flag' (from *estel*, 'star') is a non-official flag waved by Catalan independentists to express their support for an independent Catalonia from Spain. The flag dates from the early 20th century. It was born from the fusion of the four traditional red stripes of the Senyera with a triangle containing a star, inspired by the flags of Cuba and Puerto Rico. The star in the fighting flag comes from the early days of nationalism. The lone star means national freedom and independence. Cuba's fight for its independence from Spain was followed with attention by the Catalanists of the 19th century. The usage of this flag as a protest token within Catalan nationalism became more apparent ever since the 1970s Spanish transition to democracy ●

NATIONAL DAY OF CATALONIA — SEP 11TH

Crunching**numbers**

as of Jan.1st.2012

City's population	1,620,943
Population Metropolitan Area	4,798,143
Population of Catalonia	7,570,908
City's surface area	101.4 km² (39.2 sq mi)
Altitude (Pl. St. Jaume/Tibidabo)	13 m/512 m (43 ft/1680 ft)
Total length of beaches	4.58 km (2.8 mi)
Gardens and urban parks	71
Max/min average temperature	20.9°C / 15°C (70°F/59°F)
Cycle lane	186.7 km (116 mi)
Museums	67

AVERAGE NUMBER OF VISITS (%)

- 1st visit
- 2nd visit
- 3rd visit

25.7
14.8
53.7

HOTELS

7,440,113	Tourists in hotels
15,931,932	Overnight stays
352	Nbr of hotels

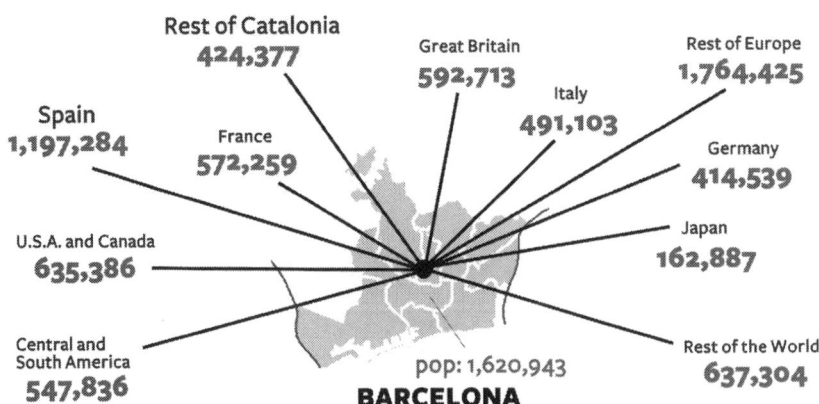

Rest of Catalonia
424,377

Great Britain
592,713

Rest of Europe
1,764,425

Italy
491,103

Spain
1,197,284

France
572,259

Germany
414,539

U.S.A. and Canada
635,386

Japan
162,887

Central and South America
547,836

Rest of the World
637,304

pop: 1,620,943
BARCELONA

WHERE DO VISITORS COME FROM...

This statistics include only tourists staying in hotels in Barcelona.
SOURCE: *Tourism statistics for Barcelona and province*—TURISME DE BARCELONA, 2013

aboutTOURISTS

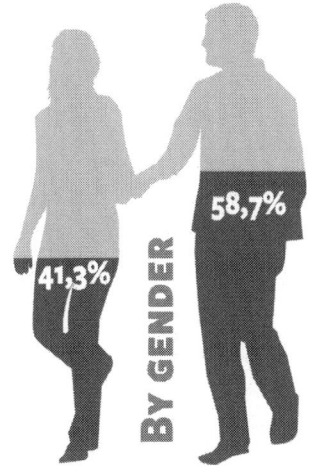

By Gender

58,7%

41,3%

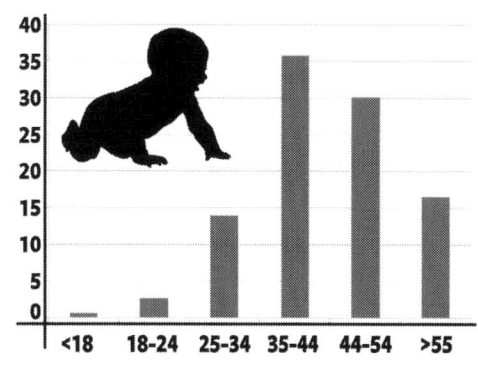

TOURISTS ACCORDING TO AGE (%)

Nbr of enquiries at tourist info desks **3,378,693**

...my conclusions

- with a ratio of over 4-to-1 visitors each year, we Barcelonians better start enlarging the kitchens in our restaurants to feed you all.
- 1/4th of visitors fall in love with the city and come over and over again.
- we have a bunch of hotels.
- guys seem to like Barcelona more than girls... c'mon girls, r u gonna take this?
- plenty of poms, scots, yankees, springboks, ozzies, kiwis, paddys and canuks makes English one of the most spoken languages among our foreign guests.
- ...and given how many inquiries are attended every year by the Tourist Information desks in the city, I'd say "boy, you do ask a lot!"

probably because many haven't got this guide book. I figure!

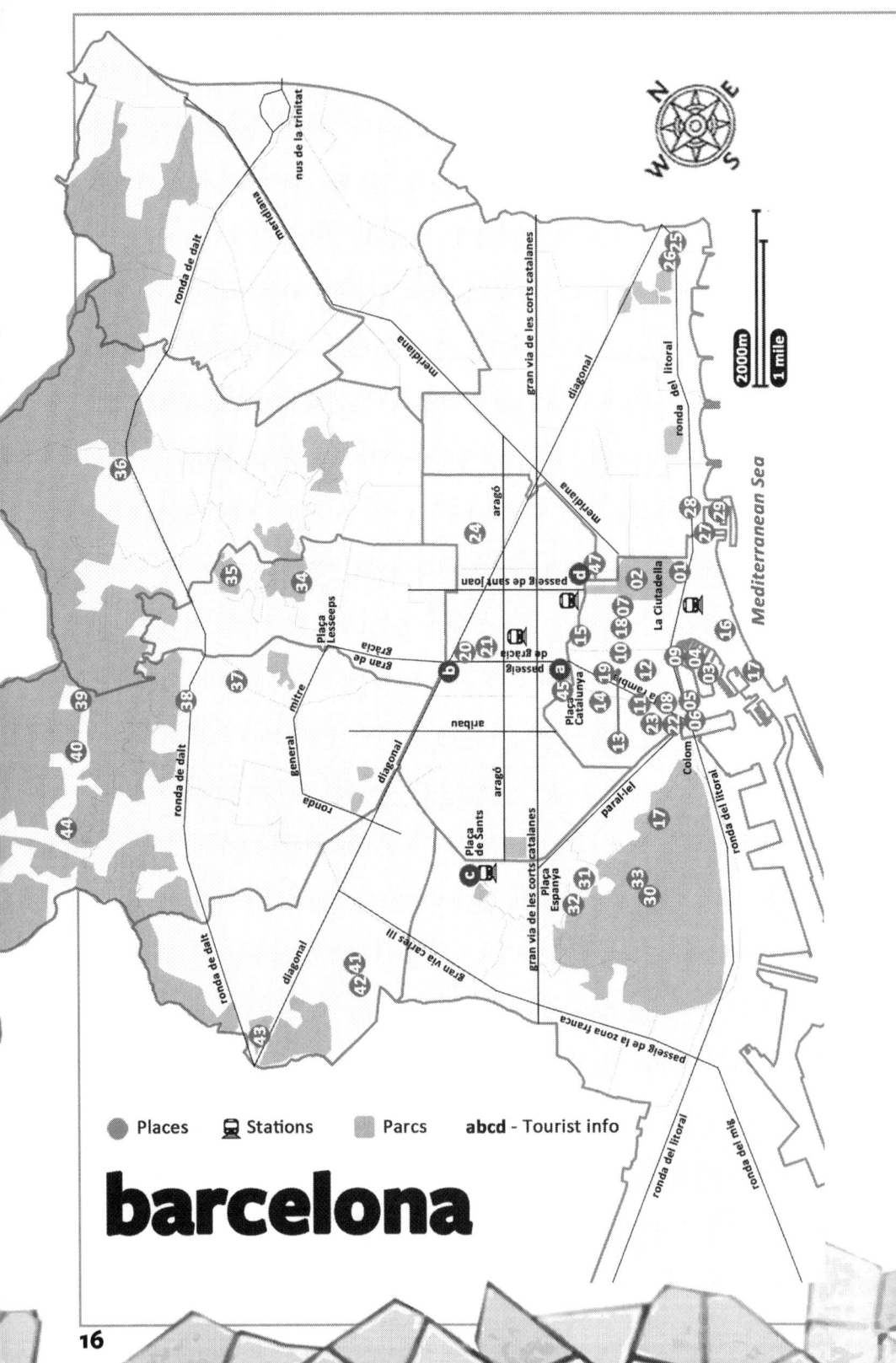

Places · Stations · Parcs · **abcd** - Tourist info

barcelona

ATTRACTIONS & ACTIVITIES

Discover fun things you can do while visiting Barcelona...

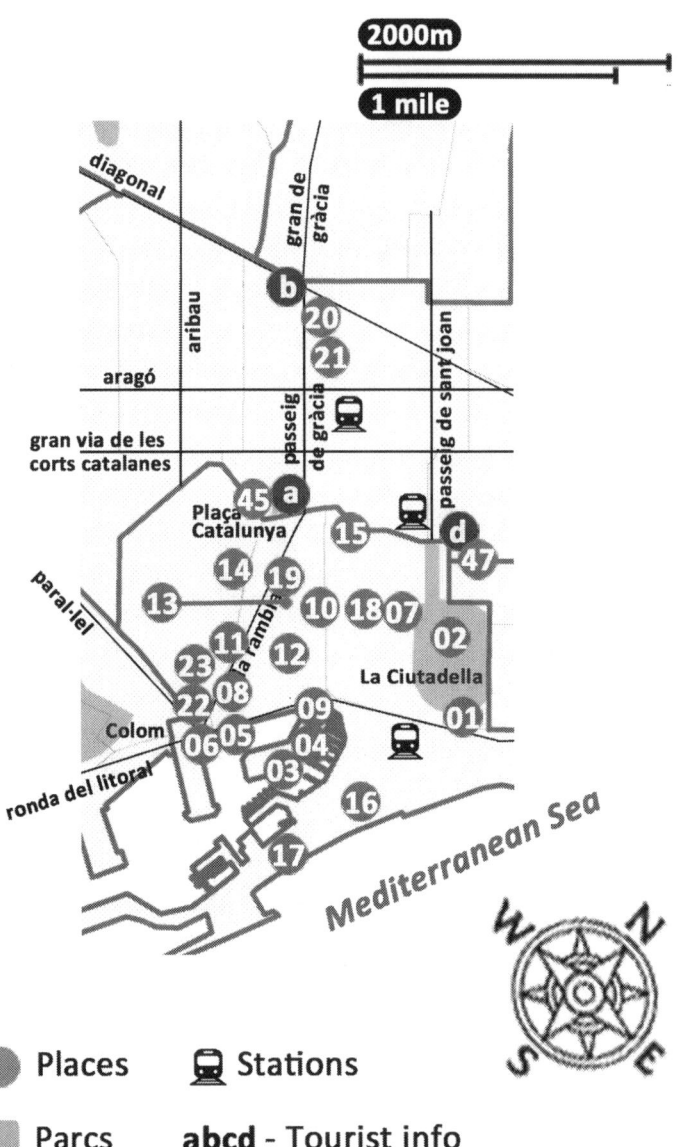

2000m

1 mile

diagonal

gran de gràcia

aribau

b

20

21

aragó

passeig de gràcia

passeig de sant joan

gran via de les corts catalanes

45

a

Plaça Catalunya

15

d

47

paral·lel

14

19

13

10 18 07

02

11

la rambla

12

23

22 08

09

La Ciutadella

01

Colom

06 05

04

03

ronda del litoral

16

17

Mediterranean Sea

W N E S

● Places   🚊 Stations

▪ Parcs   **abcd** - Tourist info

Zone Central

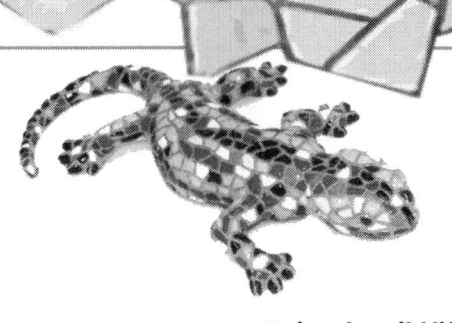

El Barri Gòtic
the heart of the city

The Barri Gòtic (*pronounced "bah-ree goh-teak"*) or Gothic Quarter is the centre of the old city of Barcelona. It stretches from La Rambla to Via Laietana, and from the Mediterranean seafront to Ronda de Sant Pere. Despite several changes undergone in the 19th and early 20th century, many of the buildings date from Medieval times, some from as far back as the Roman settlement of Barcelona. Remains of the squared Roman Wall can be seen and El Call, the medieval Jewish quarter, is located within this area too.

Combined with a wander down frenetic, commercial La Rambla, a stroll through the medieval alleyways and secluded squares of the Old City is the best possible introduction to Barcelona and the starting point for most visitors upon arrival in the city. The Barri Gòtic retains a labyrinthine street plan, with many small streets opening out into squares. Most of the quarter is closed to regular traffic although open to service vehicles and taxis.

But this is not to say that this is the only *centre* of the modern Barcelona. From the late 1700s, Barcelona grew by absorbing neighbouring villages such as Gràcia, Sants or Sarrià among others that today configure the different districts of the city. Each of these districts retained its distinct personality, traditions and celebrations thus creating a myriad of 'smaller Barcelonas' so to speak, each one with its own *centre* for social life and activities.

More recently, the celebration of two major events hosted in the city, the 1992 Olympic Games and the Universal Forum of Cultures in 2004, revived the seafront area of Barcelona by renewing and enlarging the neighbourhoods of El Poble Nou and Diagonal Mar and creating the so-called 22@ District, or the new office district of Barcelona.

In short, those looking for '*the*' centre of Barcelona will soon find out that Barcelona is a city with many facets hence many *centres* ●

Enjoy the wild life

at the ZOO DE BARCELONA

Currently housing over 7,000 animals in a 74 acre park, and former home of Snow Flake, who died in 2004.

The zoo has an area for each animal: the **Aquarama** for the dolphins; the **Komodos** for the dragons; the **Reptile House** for the poison dart frogs, the large caimans, the giant snakes and the dwarf crocodiles; the **Aviary** for the exotic birds; the **Farm** for the horses, pigs, goats, cows, rabbits and donkeys; the **Palmeral** for the parrots, cockatoos and macaws and the **Titi Monkey**

Gallery and the **Gorilla Enclosure** for... the gorillas of course.

The **Aquarama** is where the four bottle nosed dolphins from Barcelona Zoo's collection live. They give daily performances to audiences of up to 300 people. Here you can enjoy watching their acrobatics and perhaps even participate in their games. Come to meet *Nika, Leia, Anak* and *Blau!* •

wanna go there

Zoo de Barcelona
Passeig Picasso s/n - (inside the Parc de la Ciutadella)
08003 BARCELONA - Tel. 902 457 545 (local number)

L4-Barceloneta, L1-Arc de Triomf
14,39,40,41,42,51
Estació de França (Rodalies)
T4-Wellington

10am-8pm (summer), 10am-5:30pm (winter)

free

www.zoobarcelona.cat

Lat: 41.38689
Long: 2.18860

Zone CENTRAL

Betcha didn't know that...

The Barcelona Zoo also offers a whole host of activities and services which make it the perfect day out for all the family: bars and restaurants, pony rides, electric cars, shops and picnic areas. There are also several other attractions near by.

Snow Flake, who died in 2004, was the only known albino gorilla so far, and the most popular resident of the Barcelona Zoo. His original name was Nfumu Ngui in Fang language (*"white gorilla"*) by his captor, he was then nicknamed Floquet de Neu (*Catalan for "little snowflake"*) by his keeper Jordi Sabater Pi.

Nika is a female dolphin, she's 45 years old (perhaps the oldest in Europe) and she's never been ill. Lucky she! Nowadays she's retired as she cannot jump or swim as much as before, so she doesn't have any duties assigned... she exercises as she pleases and spends the day playing with other dolphins •

My advice

The dolphin show is performed daily at 11.30am, 1.30pm and 4.30pm... make sure you're there a while in advance to get the best seats.

Hire a row-boat

#02

at the PARC DE LA CIUTADELLA
pronounced "park dah lah see-oo-ta-the-lee-ah"

El Parc de la Ciutadella is one of the main green spaces in the city of Barcelona.

There are many trees, palms and bushes which are identified so visitors can recognise the main species or the most exotic, of which there are a lot. Of all the activities that you can enjoy in this park I like to highlight two of them: **biking** and **boating** on the lake. Around the park you will find various stalls where you can rent bikes to ride in the park. Once inside you will easily find the lake and a fleet of small rowing boats waiting to be led by you. There are also other facilities like a children's recreation area, a picnic area and tennis tables. Check as well the **Font de la Cascada**, a triumphal arch with waterfall and fountain with a golden quadriga on top. Find the statue of the Lady with the umbrella, she looks as if she might invite us to take her hand and stroll with her through the park gardens ●

Parc de la Ciutadella

Passeig Picasso s/n
08003 BARCELONA - Tel. +34 932 853 834 (Tourist Inf.)

 L4-Barceloneta, L1-Arc de Triomf
 14,39,40,41,42,51
 Estació de França (Rodalies)
T4-Wellington

10am–9pm (summer), 10am–6pm (winter)

  free

Zone CENTRAL

Lat: 41.38876
Long: 2.18671

www.bcn.cat/parcsijardins

wanna go there

Find the stone mammoth by the lake and get a shot while sitting on his tusks!

Betcha didn't know that...

The Ciutadella was originally an army fortress –the largest in Europe- built by King Philip V of Spain after having defeated the Catalans and entered its capital city, Barcelona, in **1714**. Its mission was to maintain stark control over the city and subdue its citizens. Hundreds of Catalans were forced to pertinaciously work on the erection for three years, while the rest of the city provided financial backing.

Finally, in 1869, most of the buildings of the much-hated fortress were eventually demolished and the remains were turned over to the city.

In 1888, Barcelona held the **Universal Exhibition of Barcelona** extravaganza (World Fair), inspired by Mayor Rius i Taulet, and the park was redesigned by addition of sculptures and other complemental works of art.

Nowadays, after a bit of political freedom was achieved in 1977, the Catalan Parliament is there •

My advice

You can spend almost half a day visiting La Ciutadella or most of a day if you include the zoo as well, there are so many things to do! Sunday is the best day to come to La Ciutadella but expect quite a few people visiting the different attractions, especially during the summer months.

Walk among sharks

#03 at the AQUARIUM DE BARCELONA

11000 marine animals from 450 different species which live in 5 million litres of water in 35 tanks.

L'Aquarium is one of Europe's biggest marine leisure and education centres. My favourite part is the **Oceanarium**, a 36 metre diameter tank, which has the most spectacular tiger sharks, giltheads, ocean sunfish, rays and sandbar sharks and most important of all... **you can walk among them**, as if you were walking on the sea bed!

For that you need to descend a series of ramps to find the underwater tunnel, 80 metres long, which will lead you through a realm you could never normally experience. Suddenly you are among the fish - perhaps not quite swimming with them - but certainly the nearest you can get to it with your clothes on •

Aquarium de Barcelona
Moll d'Espanya del Port Vell s/n- (by the Maremagnum)
08039 BARCELONA - Tel. +34 932 217 474

Ⓜ L3-Drassanes, L4-Barceloneta

🚌 19,49, Bus Turístic (stop: Port Vell)

Ⓡ

9.30am-9pm (9.30pm on week-ends and public holidays.
11pm during July and August)

www.aquariumbcn.com

Lat: 41.37680
Long: 2.18409

Zone CENTRAL

wanna go there

• •

Betcha didn't know that...

Many of the tanks at the Aquarium extend all the way to the floor, making it very stroller friendly. There's a great kids play area that's geared towards younger kids (1 to 4 y.o.) next to the cafeteria.

If you have a diving qualification you might be eligible for a dive in the Oceanarium where over 15 sharks coexist with eels, rays, dusky groupers, morays, etc. Check L'Aquarium website for more information •

• •

My advice

L'Aquarium is one of the most popular attractions in Barcelona, be ready to queu a bit to get in, especially during summer months. Alternatively you can beat the queues by pre—booking online at their website.

Feel it very close

at the IMAX PORT VELL BARCELONA

Swim with the dolphins, walk among dinosaurs, explore the pyramids, ride the magical unicorn over Africa.

See amazing films on 3D in a giant 360° screen which will totally immerse you in the movie. The larger than life sights, sounds, and overall experience whisk you away to new worlds while you remain in the comfort of your chair. It was opened in 1995, and is a relaxing way to spend some time in Barcelona.

The term 'IMAX' comes from the words 'Image Maximum' and the IMAX Experience can be described as 'the most powerful and involving film experience possible'. The difference between the IMAX Experience and watching a film at a conventional cinema is the feeling that you don't merely watch a film - **you feel as if you are actually there** - inside the human body, fighting for survival in Antarctica or plunging into the depths of the sea ●

IMAX Port Vell Barcelona
Moll d'Espanya del Port Vell s/n- (by the Maremagnum)
08039 BARCELONA - Tel. +34 932 251 111

 L3-Drassanes, L4-Barceloneta
19,49,Bus Turístic (stop: Port Vell)

12:30am-8:30pm.
(check the website for the featured films and showtimes)

www.imaxportvell.com

wanna go there

Zone CENTRAL   Lat: 41.37772
                                Long: 2.18396

Betcha didn't know that...

There are 528 IMAX theatres in 46 countries. Tiger Child was the first IMAX movie and was released in 1970.

It is projected on giant screens which extend beyond your peripheral vision -so big, in fact, that a whale can appear life-size- IMAX screens can be up to eight stories high. Because these screens fill your peripheral vision, you have the sense of being right in the action.

All manner of films are shown, and you have several choices as to how you view them. The most dramatic choice is 3D, which combines 3D technology with special glasses to give you a truly unique cinematic experience •

My advice

Please note that albeit the visual experience is spectacular by itself, the IMAX Movies are narrated in Catalan or in Spanish and are seldomly subtitled in English... still it's an impressive attraction!

Discover the city skyline

with LAS GOLONDRINAS (ferry)

pronounced "las goh-lon-<u>dree</u>-nahs"

#05

An ideal opportunity to get some fresh air while admiring the coast line of Barcelona from the sea.

It is probably the oldest nautical attraction in the city of Barcelona as its *Golondrinas* –a Spanish word meaning sparrow and a type of motorboat– started to take people by the Port on the occasion of the 1888 World Fair.

There are 2 different sailing tours to choose from: **The Barcelona port tour** which stays inside the breakwater and is essentially a tour around the port of Barcelona in a traditional *"golondrina"* and a more exciting option, **the Port and Coast tour**, which is on a bigger sea-faring catamaran. This tour leaves the port follows the coast on the open sea all the way out to Forum Harbour at the north edge of Barcelona towards Badalona •

Las Golondrinas
Plaça del Portal de la Pau s/n- (end of Les Rambles)
08001 BARCELONA - Tel. +34 934 423 106

 L3-Drassanes

 14,36,59,64,D20,Bus Turístic (stop: Colom)

11:30am-6:30pm for route BCN Port or 8:15pm for route BCN Mar
(check daily schedules in their website)

   free

www.lasgolondrinas.com

Zone CENTRAL   Lat: 41.37557
                         Long: 2.17912

wanna go there

Betcha didn't know that...

The traditional *Golondrinas* have all typical Spanish female names: María del Carmen, Encarnación and Lolita.

During prehistoric times, in the late Pliocene, the coast line of Barcelona was much further inland than it is today, in fact, a whopping 2 km! If we lived in those times the beach would be at the avenue of La Gran Via de les Corts Catalanes. It was not until the 15th century that we would find the coast line where it is today.

The port of Barcelona ranks the 9th busiest container port in Europe and the 1st in holiday cruises with over 2.6 million passengers mooring in Barcelona in 2011. Keeping in mind there are 1.8 million residents in the city itself –up to 5 in the metropolitan area– is as if every Barcelonian would have had a visitor of his own. One could call it an invasion! •

My advice

You might want to download a copy of the itinerary at "www.lasgolondrinas.com/pedeefes/escoles-2007.pdf" as there is no commentary during the trip and you might get a bit lost. Also, don't forget to take your camera with you and, if the day it's a bit cold, a sweater or a light coat.

Riding the waves

at a catamaran or in a speedboat

Experience the sea from a more unique perspective, if you feel like having a less 'touristy' ride to see Barcelona.

Catamaran Orsom, one of the largest and most modern sailing catamarans in Catalonia, capable of cruising at speeds of 16 knots. Its elegant design, stability and professional crew will give you the opportunity to experience sailing in the Mediterranean in spacious comfort and security. Enjoy a one and a half hour tour of peaceful sailing. Relax and feel the sun on your face, listen to the sound of the breeze in the sails, and watch the water lapping against the hull. And hear the silence.... shhhh! •

Catamaran Orson / Barcelona Speedboat
Moll de Drassanes - (end of Les Rambles)
08039 BARCELONA - Tel. +34 934 410 537

M L3-Drassanes
TMB 14,36,59,64,D20, Bus Turístic (stop: Colom)
R

Call for timetable as it varies every week.

▶▶ €€ €€€

Zone CENTRAL   Lat: 41.37557
Long: 2.17912

www.barcelona-orsom.com

wanna go there

Tours
last 90'
for Catamaran
Orson and 50'
for Barcelona
Speedboat.

Betcha didn't know that...

Looking for something a bit different? A more heart-pounding activity, a fun and adventurous ride on **X-Max**, a speedboat for up to 40 passengers cruising at 23 knots and speeding up to 38 knots for the most fun ride you'll probably ever have in the water. Experience the thrill and speed of **Barcelona Speedboat** in a 50 minutes ride that will take you from the Monument to Columbus to the Forum Harbour and back •

My advice

Book in advance... as it's sometimes hard to find seats, especially in summer. Booking can only be done in person at their premises... sadly not by phone nor by email. Also, from time to time, Catamaran Orson offers sunset and full moon cruises in which you can enjoy gorgeous views of the city from a totally different ambient. I've done it once and I loved it, I am sure you will too! It is ideal if you like photography. For more information call them.

Let's get dirty

at the MUSEU DE LA XOCOLATA

pronounced "moo-<u>seh</u>-oo dah lah shoo-coo-<u>lah</u>-tah"

You see, Xocolata means chocolate. And to me, good chocolate is a key ingredient of a great vacation.

The museum shows how the cocoa bean is transformed into chocolate in different historical eras. You'll also learn about chocolate's place in history and how it has been represented in media and advertising.

Chocolate is used in ways that are hard to imagine and the place is littered with amazing chocolate sculptures including various well-known Barcelona buildings –like the **Sagrada Família**-, and illustrations from various stories.

At the end is the best cafeteria in Barcelona, **the chocolate cafeteria**. It's really a gift shop but I think it has enough fresh chocolate to be considered a chocolate restaurant. Forget tapas. Have chocolate for lunch and dinner! You're on holiday. No one will know ●

Betcha didn't know that...

Chocolate is a vegetable, is derived from cocoa beans. Sugar is derived from either sugar cane or sugar beets. Both are plants, which places them in the vegetable category. Thus, chocolate is a vegetable. To go one step further, chocolate candy bars also contain milk, which is dairy. So candy bars are a health food.

Milk and white chocolate are sources of calcium. Calcium is needed to keep our bones and teeth strong.

Chocolate was originally a Mexican drink. As the story goes, shortly after arriving at Tenochtitlán (Mexico) in the fall of 1519, Hernán Cortés and the Spanish conquistadores were granted an audience with emperor Moctezuma at his breakfast table. They found the Aztec ruler sipping an exotic drink called *xocóatl* (meaning bitter water). Cacao or chocolates beans were used as currency by Aztec and Maya tribes. If we had that today we would be eating out of our wallets! •

My advice

After you've finished visiting the museum, head for Caelum (see page 176) —which is not that far away by the way— and enjoy a well deserved delicious chocolate treat!

Unravel the mysteries

of the MUSEU DE CERA
pronounced "moo-seh-oo dah seh-rah"

Ah! time has come to a standstill through some of the most prominent figures in the history of mankind. Spooky!

Musicians, painters, sculptors, clowns, artists, emperors, kings & queens, thieves, warriors, murderers, popes... and of course, the chamber of horrors! **Over 360 human-like wax figures** representing historical and entertainment personalities like Clinton, Picasso or Princess Diana. Imagine seeing Star Wars characters in person, what would you say to Luke Skywalker?

And when you're finished visiting the museum head for the **Bosc de les Fades** (*the Forest of the Fairies*), a unique and magical place: a forest inhabited by strange trees, gnomes, fairies and other unexpected creatures where you will be able to have a refreshment while discovering the secrets that this place can offer •

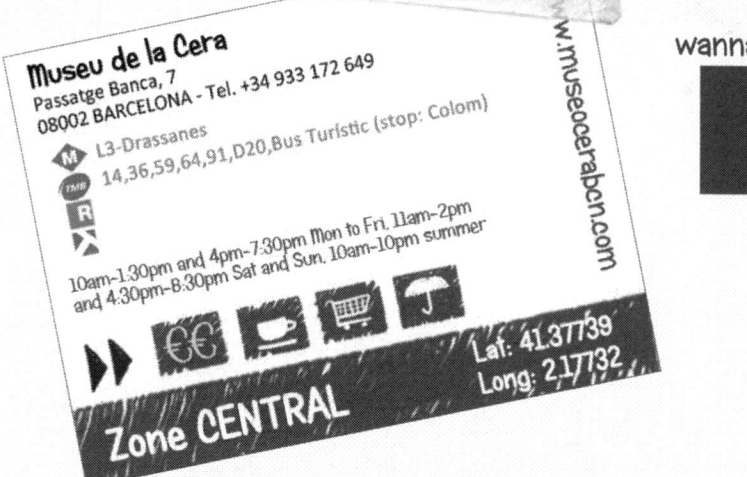

Museu de la Cera
Passatge Banca, 7
08002 BARCELONA - Tel. +34 933 172 649

M L3-Drassanes
TMB 14,36,59,64,91,D20,Bus Turístic (stop: Colom)
R
▶◀

10am-1:30pm and 4pm-7:30pm Mon to Fri. 11am-2pm and 4:30pm-8:30pm Sat and Sun. 10am-10pm summer

Lat: 41.37739
Long: 2.17732

Zone CENTRAL

www.museoceraben.com

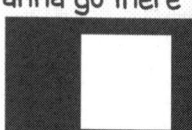

wanna go there

Betcha didn't know that...

A good picture, the perfect souvenir. Get a fantastic picture of a different Barcelona with you as the protagonist. The museum offers the possibility to have your picture taken in amazing scenarios.

The Passatge del Temps is another attraction of the museum that will captivate you with its cutting-edge design and comfortable atmosphere, while offering an innovative take on the ancient art of origami.

Tip: when you're at the inside patio facing the entrance before entering the museum... turn around and look up, you'll see a special wax character 'greeting' the visitors. Guess who is that? •

My advice

Tickets can be bought in advance via their online payment system. Note that part of the process is in Spanish only but it is intuitive enough to follow.

Learn and play
at the MUSEU D'HISTÒRIA DE CATALUNYA

pronounced "moo-seh-oo dees-toh-ree-ah dah ca-tah-loo-neeah"

From its first inhabitants some 450,000 years ago to the present, the memory of a country: Catalonia.

The influx of eastern societies, led into the development of **Iberian culture**, one of the most important civilisations of the western Mediterranean. In 218 BC a long period of links with the **Roman Empire** began until the 5th century. In 711, the Muslim army began its conquest and a new country -**al-Andalus**- came into being. The establishment of the **Carolingian Empire** signalled the transition to the Middle Ages and the future Catalonia began its reconstruction under its protection. By the 10th century territorial expansion took place and the breaking of ties with the Frankish signed the birth of **the country of Catalonia**. Then, many other things happened until the present day: conquests, discoveries, defeats... but why don't you find them for yourself at the museum? You'll enjoy it! •

Museu d'Història de Catalunya
Plaça de Pau Vila, 3 (Palau de Mar)
08003 BARCELONA - Tel. +34 932 254 700

M L4-Barceloneta
17,36,39,40,45,59,64,D20,Bus Turístic
R

10am-7pm Tue to Sat (2:30pm on Sun and public holidays)

€ free

Zone CENTRAL
Lat: 41.38095
Long: 2.18574

www.mhcat.net

wanna go there

Betcha didn't know that...

"Catalan" is the local language of Catalonia, where Barcelona is its capital. It's developed from Latin and it's similar to French, Italian and Spanish. Aranese is also spoken in the northwest of Catalonia.

During the Middle Ages, as part of the Crown of Aragon, the Catalans became a maritime power, expanding by trade and conquest into Valencia, the Balearic Islands, and even Sardinia and Sicily and establishing consulates as far as London, Lisboa, Alexandria, Beirut or modern day Istanbul.

The defeat of Catalan troops on Sept. 11th, 1714 during the War of the Spanish Succession, marked the end of the Catalan independence when Spanish king Felipe V of Bourbon banned all the main Catalan political institutions, language and imposed military-based rule over the region •

My advice

There are many things to see and to do in this museum. Expect to spend many hours here. If you get tired you can go to rest to the "1881 Restaurant Coffee Shop" in the fourth floor. It has a terrace which oversees the habour. Excellent choice during the summer months.

Living like the ancient Romans

at the MUHBA

The Barcelona City History Museum (MUHBA) takes you a journey through Barcelona's 2500 year history.

Just a few floors under the current Barcelona city level you will find yourself in the ruins of **Barcino**, the Roman city of Barcelona. See the remains of the first city wall, its streets, craft workshops and the episcopal buildings.

On the **Plaça del Rei**, where the central Barcelona History museum is located, you can also visit a series of splendid monuments which provide an insight into medieval Barcelona: the *Palau Reial Major,* a medieval royal palace with Romanesque vaulted chambers, the *Saló del Tinell* great hall –this majestic room began life in 1370 as the seat of the Catalan parliament and was converted in the 18th century into a Baroque church, which was dismantled in 1934, the *Capella de Santa Àgata* and the watchtower *Torre del Rei Martí* •

MUHBA – Museu d'Història de la Ciutat
Plaça del Rei, s/n
08002 BARCELONA - Tel. +34 932 562 100

L4-Jaume I, L3-Liceu
17,19,40,45,Bus Turístic (stop: Barri Gòtic)

10am–7pm Tue to Sat (April to October, until 5pm rest of the year). Until 8pm on Sun.

free

Lat: 41.38398
Long: 2.17788

Zone CENTRAL

Betcha didn't know that...

The name Barcelona comes from the ancient Iberian Phoenician *"Barkeno"*. Sources say that the city could have been named after the Carthaginian general Hamilcar Barca, who is supposed to have founded the city in the 3rd century BC.

About 15 BC, the Romans redrew the town as a *castrum* (Roman military camp) naming it *"Iulia Augusta Faventia Paterna Barcino"* and it was mostly intended for veterans of the army. Under the Romans,

Barcino enjoyed immunity from imperial burdens and minted its own coins.

Between the chapel and the museum entrance at the Plaça del Rei there is a glass door, is the access to the house of the executioner during the Middle Ages. The job of executioner was respected and feared in equal measure. He had to exist but no one wanted to have much relationship with such a character •

My advice

Get a combined ticket for all sites MUHBA. You can then visit as well: Temple d'August, Via Sepulcral Romana, Domus i Sitges, El Call, Santa Caterina, Monastir de Pedralbes, Vil.la Joana, Refugi 307 and the Casa del Guarda at Parc Guell. Check the website for more information.

Watch street performers

at the lower end of LA RAMBLA

pronounced "lah ram-blah"

You will be able to say that you have made even statues talk! A miracle? or is it because you're sooooo good?...

One of the major attractions of walking down Barcelona's main street, La Rambla, is watching the numerous street performers, most of which are **human statues**. Everybody, even adults but most especially children are astounded by the variety of costumes on show, which make the most famous road in Barcelona such a characteristic place. From the morning to the evening, and especially during the more 'touristy' times of day, you can witness them in astounding numbers provoking a spontaneous curiosity to know what is hiding behind the mask.

A little tip: bring all your loose change (put it aside especially) so you can give a little to each of the ones you see. They will appreciate this and will usually put on 'a little show' for you and let you take a picture of them •

La Rambla
08001/08002 BARCELONA

- **M** L3-Liceu, L3-Drassanes, L6 and L7-Catalunya (FGC)
- **TMB** 14,16,17,41,42,55,59,91,D20,Bus Turístic (stop: Col
- **R** Plaça Catalunya (Rodalies)

The human statues are performing most of the day, every day.

▶▶  free

Zone CENTRAL Lat: 41.37719
Long: 2.17841

Betcha didn't know that...

La Rambla has in fact a group of different sections and that is why it is also usually called in plural: Les Rambles. From Plaça Catalunya the various sections have the following names: *Rambla Canaletes, Rambla dels Estudis, Rambla de Sant Josep, Rambla dels Caputxins* and *Rambla de Santa Mònica*.

For many centuries, La Rambla had been the centre of the city and that's why it has so many important buildings near by. In La Rambla itself you can find: the monument to Columbus, several palaces and noble buildings, the market of La Boqueria, the Grand Teatre del Liceu... and the Font de Canaletes –where all the FC Barcelona fans go to celebrate the winning of the football league! ●

My advice

La Rambla is a very busy street and there are pickpockets and beggars operating in the area: watch your belongings at all times. Yes, of course, that should include your parents too!

Walk about in the oldest part of town

at the BARRI GÒTIC

pronounced "bah-ree goh-teak"

12

The Barri Gòtic is the birthplace of Barcelona and has always been the centre of its social and political life.

The **Barri Gòtic** (*Gothic quarter*) –roughly 1km x 0.5km– is so called because it used to be the Roman village and thus has some remnants of its glorious past. The narrow, winding streets create quite a labyrinth and means that it may take a while to get your bearings. I recommend that you should always look up and around you or you may miss some of the best bits.

The Gothic quarter has many peaceful corners where you can relax and enjoy your surroundings away from the busy shopping streets. Two of the main attractions, right in the heart of the district, are the huge **Cathedral of the Holy Cross and Saint Eulàlia** which has a stunning courtyard full of plants and oddly geese and the Basilica of **Santa Maria del Mar** •

L3-Plaça Catalunya,L4-Jaume I, L6 and L7-Catalunya (FGC
 14,16,17,19,41,42,45,55,59,91,120,D20
Plaça Catalunya (Rodalies), Estació de França (Rodalies)

▶▶ free

Zone CENTRAL

Lat: 41.38272
Long: 2.17690

Betcha didn't know that...

You will be spoilt for choice of places to grab a bite and shopping is also amazing, from the more commercial area of Portal de l'Angel to all the little boutiques on Avinyó. Make sure you walk around to experience all you can, the Gothic quarter is perfect for that afternoon stroll.

Around 1650, between the Guerra dels Segadors (*Reapers' War*) against the Spanish troops of Philip IV and the black plague, Barcelona lost between 15 and 20% of its population.

During the Middle Ages Barcelona had the tallest building in Europe: the watchtower Torre del Rei Martí at la Plaça del Rei. Try counting the stairs to the top!

Picasso lived and worked in Barri Gòtic from 1895 to 1904 and Joan Miró was born and lived here during his youth ●

My advice

Should you feel compelled to sit down a have a drink and a bite, try the numerous bars and restaurants in the small streets rather than the most touristy in La Rambla and other major streets. Your parents' pocket will also thank you!

See the 'sneakers' of the ancients

at the MUSEU DEL CALÇAT

pronounced "moo-seh-oo dahl cal-sat"

The Museu del Calçat (Shoe Museum), a whimsical tour through the world of footwear.

Housed in what was once part of the **medieval shoemakers' guild premises,** this quirky little museum details the cobbler's craft, from practical Roman and Egyptian sandals and dainty ladies' shoes of the 18th century to tottering '70s platform boots.

This small collection concentrates on the craft, with sandals, plenty of *espardenyas* (Catalan peasant shoes) and a few pairs of celebrity footwear as well as some of the traditional tools, machinery and leather used in the shoemakers' trade. •

Museu del Calçat
Plaça de Sant Felip Neri, 5
08002 BARCELONA - Tel. +34 933 014 533

L3-Liceu, L4-Jaume I,

14,17,19,40,45,59,Bus Turístic (stop: Barri Gòtic)

11am–2pm Tue to Sun and public holidays.

free

Zone CENTRAL   Lat: 41.38355
                    Long: 2.17477

Betcha didn't know that...

One of the highlights of the museum is an enormous shoe which was made to fit the foot of the statue of Columbus near the port. The shoe is listed in the Guinness Book of Records as the largest shoe in the world.

The earlier examples of the museum are reproductions, while those from the 17th century to the present day are originals, including clogs, swagged musketeers' boots

Cave drawings from more than 15,000 years ago show humans with animal skins or furs wrapped around their feet.

The body of a well-preserved "ice-man" nearly 5,000 years old wears leather foot coverings stuffed with straw. Shoes, in some form or another, have been around for a very long time.

The most expensive pair of shoes in the World were created by Stuart Weitzman who designed the satin open toe stilettos around a pair of earrings owned by movie legend Rita Hayworth. The earrings are laden with rubies, sapphires and diamonds... and they cost over 3,000,000.-€ •

Visit a
colourful market
at the LA BOQUERIA
pronounced "lah booh-ke-ree-ah"

14

At La Boqueria people eat, shop and gossip together living life well and enjoying a sense of community.

The first mention of **La Boqueria** market in Barcelona dates from 1217, when tables were installed near the old city gate to sell meat. From December 1470 onwards, a pig market was held at this site. Later, the authorities decided to construct a separate market on La Rambla, housing mainly fishmongers and butchers.

Nowadays, La Boqueria is one of the **largest farmer's market in Europe** where you can find the best products from Catalonia in one place: fruit, vegetables, fish and seafood... and tapas bars like El Quim and others ●

Mercat de Sant Josep de la Boqueria
La Rambla, 91
08001 BARCELONA - Tel. +34 934 121 315

 L3-Liceu
14,59,91,Bus Turístic (stop: Barri Gòtic)

8am–8:30pm Mon to Sat

www.boqueria.info

Zone CENTRAL Lat: 41.38198 Long: 2.17218

At the main entrance, from La Rambla, you'll find to your right and left the most colourful display of fruits and vegetables you've probably ever seen.

Betcha didn't know that...

La Boqueria is a paradise for the senses. Wake to the smells and colours of La Boqueria. A multitude of feelings that open up between the noisy comings and goings of people struggling in the job of buying and selling food. And candy, chocolate and sweets too!

Pinocchio is indeed one of the mythical characters of children's literature, but I am referring here to a magical place at the entrance to La Boqueria: bar Pinocho. Juanito, the alma mater of the place, is one of the essential people in Barcelona. Breakfast at seven o'clock with tripe, fried whitebait *fricandó* would be a must for anyone who wants to know Barcelona. But if you do not want to go at seven, is open until four in the afternoon or so.

Barcelona has a staggering total of 40 steel hangar-covered open-air markets. Almost every borough has at least one if not more. Although similar in their brightly illuminated and colourful displays of vegetables, spices, mushrooms, fruits, meats, cheeses, fish and seafood, each of these markets has its own distinctive flavour and architectural personality •

My advice

This market gets extremely crowded. Do not loose sight of your parents. Hold hands!

Enter a magical auditorium

at the PALAU DE LA MÚSICA

pronounced "pa-lah-oo dah lah moo-see-ca ca-ta-lah-na"

15

Breathless! the most beautiful concert hall in the World. I'm sure you've never seen anything like this before.

Opened in 1908, this is one of the most representative buildings of **Catalan Modernist style**. Full of light and of colour, is also today, a cultural asset that is open to the world, whose halls and areas host concerts of all genres and styles, cultural and social events. The design of the Palau is typical of Catalan modernism in that curves predominate over straight lines, dynamic shapes are preferred over static forms, and rich decoration that emphasizes floral and other organic motifs is used extensively.

Over 500 concerts, more than 4,000 architectural tours with over 180,000 visitors, 32,000 students in school visits, nearly 400,000 attendees at concerts... and all these only in one season! Isn't it being 'popular' or what? •

Palau de la Música Catalana
Palau de la Música, 4-6
08003 BARCELONA - Tel. 902 442 882 (local number)

L1-Urquinaona, L4-Urquinaona
17,19,40,45,Bus Turístic (stop: Barri Gòtic)

Guided tours on the hour from 9:30am-9pm (almost) every day except certain public holidays and when coinciding with concerts. Check before visiting.

Zone CENTRAL   Lat: 41.38733
Long: 2.17541

www.palaumusica.org

wanna go there

Betcha didn't know that...

The concert hall inside has seats arranged in three levels. The stained glass skylight is a masterpiece and is in the shape of an enormous drop of light. On the sides of the stage are huge sculptures of a winged horse, three muses called the Flowers of May, and the Valkyries. The back of the stage has 18 sculptures of women playing historical musical instruments. Also, there are about 2000 large ceramic roses in different colours that adorn the ceiling.

The Palau de la Música Catalana was financed primarily by the society, but important financial contributions also were made by Barcelona's wealthy industrialists and bourgeoisie. The Palau won the architect an award from the Barcelona City Council in 1909, given to the best building built during the previous year •

My advice

Since cameras are not allowed —what a pity!— there is a very good museum store where one can buy a booklet about the palace to remember all its decorative details. Also, tickets for the tours can be purchased as of one week before the day of the tour. Advanced ticket purchase is recommended.

Relax at the beach district

#16

in LA BARCELONETA

pronounced "la bar-sah-loo-net-ah"

Nothing says vacation like white-sand beaches and luxurious indulgence... and a nice paella for lunch!

There is no need to escape to the Caribbean, we have **La Barceloneta**! Founded in 1753, when the first stone on land won to the sea was laid. The first settlers from this new neighbourhood were mainly fishermen, that due to its proximity to the sea began to build their homes here.

Today the neighbourhood still has the air of small town, although now, the 2km of fine sandy beaches are filled with summer tourists that play, sunbath, swim, or simply relax. And it's all at a stone's throw away from the centre of the city.

But not only the sea and the beach define La Barceloneta, **a myriad of restaurants**, both in the small streets and in the beach front extend along the sand. Enjoy a true fishermen's meal, from the very humble to the most opulent menus ●

La Barceloneta, the district of
08003 BARCELONA - Tel. +34 932 853 834 (Tourist Inf.)

L4-Barceloneta, L4-Ciutadella/Vil·la Olímpica
17,36,39,45,59,64,D20,Bus Turístic

www.labarceloneta.es

free

Zone CENTRAL

Lat: 41.37514
Long: 2.18971

wanna go there

Betcha didn't know that...

Until well into the sixties, the beach at La Barceloneta was the place where thousands of people lived in shacks, many arrived with the immigration of the 1920s, among them a large gypsy community. Now the beach front has several luxury hotels and top-end apartments.

The bars at La Barceloneta are widely known for their "*tapes*" –in Catalan- or "tapas" –in Spanish. The most typical is questionably the spicy potato *bomba* (bomb), according to some urban legends, it was invented at the old bar La Cova Fumada, at Carrer Baluard, 56 •

My advice

Need to take a shower after the beach? rent a locker? a towel?... check Espai de Mar at Porxos del Passeig Marítim, 5 at the beachfront in La Barceloneta or contact them by phone +34 932 214 989 or via their website at www.espaidemar.cat

17

Ride to the top of the hill

on the cable cars of Barcelona

The city has two cable cars, one crossing the old harbour and the other one taking you to the top of Montjuïc hill.

The **Transbordador Aeri del Port** is the most spectacular ride with stunning views of all Barcelona in a cable car ride that takes you across the old harbour to and from the Montjuïc hill to the beach in the Barceloneta neighbourhood. There's also a middle station, called Jaume I, a tower on a quay near the monument to Columbus.

The **Teleferic de Montjuïc** cable car starts from the middle of Montjuïc hill, there is a midway stop at the **Mirador del Alcalde** observation deck and it ends in the old military fort at the top of Montjuïc. The new gondola cars have great views of the city. Afraid of highs anyone? •

Next to the Mirador del Alcalde you'll find a monument to the Sardana (is a type of circle dance typical of Catalonia). Get in the circle and pretend to be another dancer!

Transbordador Aeri

Passeig de Joan de Borbó 88, 1
08039 BARCELONA - Tel. +34 9

 17,39,64

Every 15 minutes. from 11am-5:30pm and 7pm/8pm the rest of the year

Zone CENTRAL

Lat: 41.37324
Long: 2.18809

elona.com

wanna go there

Teleferic de Montjuic

Av. Miramar s/n, Parc de Montjuïc station
08038 BARCELONA - Tel. +34 933 187 074 Cust.Service TMB

 L2-Paral·lel, L3-Paral·lel and then Funicular
55,150,Bus Turístic (stop: Teleferic de Montjuïc)

10am-8pm/7pm depending on the season. In summer (Jun to Sep) closes at 9pm. Closed 24Jan-12Feb.

Zone CENTRAL

Lat: 41.37101
Long: 2.17243

www.tmb.cat

• • • • • • • • • • •
For those that like figures and stats: the cabins at the Transbordador Aeri del Port hold 19 persons and are 70m above the sea. The journey takes 10'. The Teleferic de Montjuïc cable car ride is 752 metres in length with an elevation of 85.5 metres. The journey takes 8' •
• • • • • • • • • • •

My advice

On your way back from the fort at the top of Montjuic stop at the Mirador del Alcalde to admire a different perspective from Barcelona. Since it's downhill I'd recommend to walk instead of taking the teleferic.

Stare a mammoth in the eye

at the MUSEU DEL MAMUT

pronounced "moo-seh-oo dahl mah-moot"

Travel back to the time when Ice Age mammoth and other giant animals roamed the land.

In the past, when ancient Catalans dug out gigantic bones they presumed these were remains of the Trojan War heroes. Later on, during the Middle Ages and up to the 19th century they were mistaken for giants -as described in the Bible- who died during the Genesis Flood. Naturally, most of these bones belonged to entirely different creatures ...**mammoths**!

While woolly mammoths were not noticeably taller than present-day African elephants, they were larger and heavier and had extremely long tusks which were markedly curved. They used them to clear the snow from ground and reach for the vegetation buried below. A mammoth's diet consisted primarily of grasses, sedges, and rushes •

Museu del Mamut
Montcada, 1
08003 BARCELONA - Tel. +34 932 688 520

Ⓜ L4-Jaume I
🚍 17,19,40,45,120,Bus Turístic (stop: Barri Gòtic)

10am–8pm (winter) and 9pm (summer)

▶▶ 💶 free 🛒

Zone CENTRAL   Lat: 41.38581
                 Long: 2.18028

www.museodelmamut.com

wanna go there

Betcha didn't know that...

This pocket-size museum was open in 2010, just two years after the most recent Ice Age remains in Southern Europe were discovered in the form of some 400 animal fragments unearthed in the seaside town of Viladecans, 5km south of Barcelona.

Everything mammoth is big: it's believed that an adult specimen ate around 300kg of food each day, drank 160 litres of water and produced over 180kg of dung per day!

The word "mammoth" comes from Russian and means 'very big'. Indeed! Mammoths vanished from most of Europe about 8,000 BC.

In May 2007, the carcass of a female woolly mammoth was discovered under the snow near the Yuribei River in Russia, where it had been buried for 37,000 years. She was a 1-month-old baby that walked the tundra and then died mysteriously. Scientists named her Lyuba ●

My advice

They have guides available in several languages at the information desk. It's a very small museum but cozy and kinda casual... If you call in advance you can book a private tour in English —for peanuts, truly, darn cheap!— Bear in mind it may be a bit informal so be understanding.

Be the mayor for a day

#19 at the AJUNTAMENT DE BARCELONA

pronounced "ah-joon-tah-men dah bar-sah-lo-nah"

A building full of history where you can be part of it. Hundreds of years of power struggles and intrigue...

The Barcelona City Hall is an institution dating back to the 13th century when King James I granted the city the right to choose the councillors and advisers and formed the **Consell de Cent** (Council of One Hundred). Around the left-hand corner of the City Hall's rather dull 18th century neo-classical façade sits the old entrance, in a wonderfully flamboyant 15th century façade. Inside, the building's centrepiece (and oldest part) is the famous **Saló de Cent**, where the Consell de Cent ruled the city between 1372 and 1714. See the Mayor's office, the Hall of the Queen Regent –the Public Chamber where sessions are celebrated– and the magnificent Saló de Cent, once the true centre of power of Barcelona. Can you feel the power and the fame already? •

Ajuntament de Barcelona
Plaça Sant Jaume, s/n
08002 BARCELONA - Tel. +34 934 027 000

Ⓜ L3-Liceu, L4-Jaume I
🚌 14,17,19,40,45,59,91,120, Bus Turístic (stop: B.Gòtic)
Ⓡ
🚶

www.bcn.cat

10am-1.30pm every SUNDAY except on public holidays.
On Feb 12th and April 23rd –local festivities– is open most
of the day.

▶▶ free ☂

Zone CENTRAL

Lat: 41.38272
Long: 2.17690

wanna go there

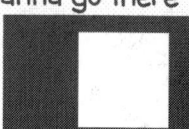

Betcha didn't know that...

El *Consell de Cent* (Council of One Hundred) was formed by nobles, master craftsmen and the richest merchants of the city and it had the mission to govern the city of Barcelona. They had two other bodies that assisted them: the *Trentena de Guerra* (The 30 of the War), responsible for coordinating the defence the city in case of attack and the *Trenta Clauers* (The 30 Keymasters), responsible for opening the gates of the city walls.

The Saló de Cent opened in 1373, has a tiled motifs representing the guilds of the city and the walls are covered with tapestries representing the flag of Catalonia: four red stripes on a gold (yellow) background. This incomparable setting was the first proto democratic municipal parliament (dating from 1274) in Europe●

My advice

You can visit the City Hall at your own pace —pick up a leaflet at the entrance!— or in a free guided tour in several languages. The tour in English starts at 11am. Take your camera, it's worth it! Also, next to the City Hall, in Carrer Ciutat, 7 you'll find the Museum of Inventions (MIBA) an ideal retreat for visiting with kids.

See a weird house

at LA PEDRERA

pronounced "lah pah-dre-rah"

La Pedrera –Catalan for quarry– is the nickname for a building formally known as Casa Milà.

A very famous buildings designed by **Gaudí**. It has a roof with a few chimneys that look like giant warriors and skylights. The loft has 270 arches placed in a structure similar to that of a skeleton. One of the apartments in the building can also be visited. It's preserved as families lived in the 1920s. How cool must it have been to live in a museum!

The unusual forms of Casa Milà has caught the attention of numerous artists, writers... and also filmmakers. La Pedrera has been used as a natural location in many movies. From the façade to the top roof to the rooms and stairs, La Pedrera is like **a huge fairy tale house** •

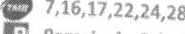

Casa Milà – La Pedrera

Provença, 261-265
08008 BARCELONA - Tel. 902 202 138 (local number)

 L3 and L5-Diagonal, L6 and L7-Provença (FGC)

7,16,17,22,24,28

Passeig de Gràcia (Rodalies)

9am–8pm Mon to Sun (March to October and until 6.30pm the rest of the year). Closed 25/Dec. and from 7 to 13/Jan.

Zone CENTRAL   Lat: 41.39528
                  Long: 2.16200

www.lapedrera.com

wanna go there

From the centre of the atrium of Casa Milà. looking upwards... what a view!

Betcha didn't know that...

The building is part of the UNESCO World Heritage Site "Works of Antoni Gaudí". The building is now owned by Catalunya Caixa, a bank corporation.

Gaudí wanted the people who lived in the flats to all know each other therefore there were only lifts on every second floor so people had to communicate with one another on different floors.

La Pedrera it is imbued in the spirit of the Modernisme, a style that emerged in the late 19th century and which was also known throughout Europe as Art Nouveau. This was the age when the architecture of Barcelona drew its inspiration from and contributed to that of Brussels, Milan, Vienna, Glasgow and Riga among other •

My advice

Busy, busy, busy... you'll queue a bit, but it's worth it. Afterwards, visit Palau Robert which is very close, an old palace that offers free exhibitions and events: art, cinema, photography, etc. and it also houses a Tourist Office. It has an inside garden: ideal to take a break from the noise of the city.

See a real mummy

at the MUSEU EGIPCI

pronounced "moo-seh-oo ah-jeep-see"

Do you know why were Ancient Egyptians mummified? Who did they actually mummify? How was the whole ritual?

The Egyptian state, which emerged on the banks of the Nile, was governed and led by individuals invested with great power: **the Pharaohs**.

King Tutankhamun is probably the best known of all of them because, unlike many tombs discovered in Egypt, his was found mostly intact. The Egyptians conceived death on earth as a provisional interruption, since human beings could live forever. In ritual terms, **the mummification** of the body was the process that conditioned, to a large extent, the possibility of eternal life.

A visit to the various halls of the **Museu Egipci** (yes, you guessed right: Egyptian Museum!) will give you a good insight of the ritual of mummification in Ancient Egypt as well as the secrets of the Pharaohs own mummies •

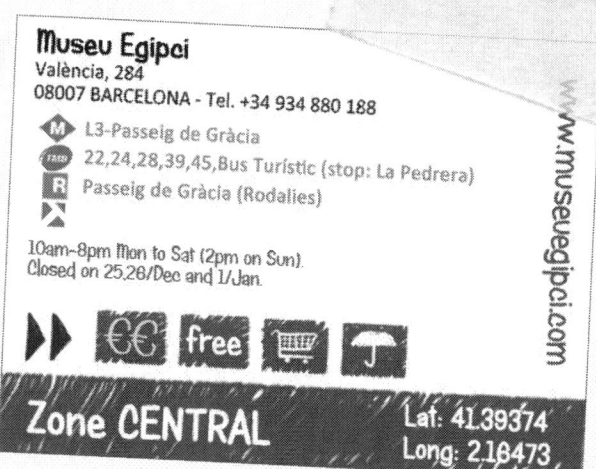

Museu Egipci
València, 284
08007 BARCELONA - Tel. +34 934 880 188

Ⓜ L3-Passeig de Gràcia

🚌 22,24,28,39,45,Bus Turístic (stop: La Pedrera)

Ⓡ Passeig de Gràcia (Rodalies)

10am–8pm Mon to Sat (2pm on Sun).
Closed on 25,26/Dec and 1/Jan.

▶▶ €€ free 🛒 ☂

Zone CENTRAL

Lat: 41.39374
Long: 2.16473

www.museuegipci.com

wanna go there

Betcha didn't know that...

Very few people in ancient Egypt could read or write, perhaps as few as 2%. The people who could were called scribes. Scribes learned the skill of writing in the schools of Egypt, which were called "Houses of Life", or "Per Ankh". It was a very difficult skill to learn, as the Egyptians had more than 500 hieroglyphic signs in their written language.

One of the keys to unlocking the secrets of ancient Egyptian writing was the 'Rosetta Stone', a stone with writing on it created in 196 BC. It was discovered in a town called Rosetta, on the Mediterranean coast in Egypt. The text is made up of three translations of a single passage, written in two Egyptian language scripts (hieroglyphic and Demotic), and in classical Greek. The Rosetta Stone was found in 1799 by French soldiers who were rebuilding a fort. It took twenty years for scholars to decode the slab!.

The Ancient Egyptians believed that the brain did not serve any purpose in the afterlife. During the mummification process, the brain was liquefied by metal instruments and removed through the nose. Ergh! •

Arr! batten down the hatches

at the **MUSEU MARÍTIM**

pronounced "moo-seh-oo mah-ree-team"

This museum is housed in the Drassanes Reals, the former royal shipyards, built between 1283 and 1328.

Among the museum's fascinating array of artefacts there are ships of all shapes and sizes, dioramas and maps and things that they discovered and brought back to Europe from the Americas. The centrepiece of the museum is **a huge full-size replica of Juan de Austria's Lepanto galley**, used in 1571 against the Moors. On board, you get a brief 3D virtual reality show of the crew - chained four-by-four to their benches for months on end. You could smell these things two miles away, you could smell them before you could see them, it was said. Many of the crew were Turkish slaves, prisoners of war •

Museu Marítim - Les Drassanes
Av. de les Drassanes s/n
08001 BARCELONA - Tel. +34 933 429 920

L3-Drassanes
14,36,59,64,91,D20,120,Bus Turístic (stop: Colom)

www.mmb.cat

Tue to Sun 10am-5:30pm (winter) and 8:30pm (summer). On Sat opens at 2pm. The pailebot Santa Eulàlia sails on Saturday morning (summer) and Monday morning (winter).

free

Lat: 41.37642
Long: 2.17450

Zone CENTRAL

wanna go there

Betcha didn't know that...

The Drassanes were built in 1243 are were built as a galley arsenal in the service of the Crown of Aragon.

During the Middle Ages, when it came to enforce the law, the affairs of the sea were dealt with by the Consolat del Mar (Consulate of the Sea) instead of the ordinary courts. Its members were aristocrats with experience in commercial matters and good reputation in the community.

Formerly, standing in the port, and part of the museum, there was also a full-size replica of the Santa Maria on which Columbus sailed in 1492, but it was thought politically expedient to quietly sink it. It's now apparently up the coast off the Illes Medes, no gold on board, sorry! •

My advice

And the most exciting feature yet: the fleet. Visit four small modern boats: Polux, Drac, Lola and Catapum and the magnificent pailebot, a small schooner without topsails, named Santa Eulàlia. Immerse yourself in history and discover the rich maritime traditions of the Mediterranean!

See how rich people used to live

at the PALAU GÜELL

pronounced "pah-lah-oo goo-ehl"

#23

A palace in the heart of the city where you'll see how the rich and spoiled used to live in the early 1900s.

Eusebi Güell, 1st Count of Güell was a Catalan patriarch who profited greatly from the industrial revolution in Catalonia in the late 19th Century. He became patron to architect Antoni Gaudí from whom Güell commissioned the **Palau Güell**, his permanent residence.

The ornate walls and ceilings of the receiving room disguised small viewing windows high on the walls where the owners of the home could view their guests from the upper floor and get a 'sneak peek' before greeting them. The main party room has a high ceiling with small holes near the top where lanterns were hung at night from the outside to give the appearance of a starlit sky. Feeling rich and influential already? •

Palau Güell
Nou de la Rambla, 3-5
08001 BARCELONA - Tel. +34 934 725 775 / 771

L3-Liceu, L3-Drassanes
14,59,91,Bus Turístic (stop: Barri Gòtic)

From 10am-8pm Tue to Sun (April 1st to Oct 31st).
to 5.30pm the rest of the year.

free

Zone CENTRAL   Lat: 41.37923
Long: 2.17442

www.palauguell.cat

Take a few pictures of yourself in the different rooms of the palace to brag with your friends back home.

Betcha didn't know that...

The Palau Güell is centered on a main room for entertaining high society guests. Guests entered the home in horse drawn carriages through the front iron gates, which featured a parabolic arch and intricate patterns of forged iron-work resembling seaweed and in some parts a horsewhip.

The roof terrace has several chimneys and ventilation towers decorated in a type of mosaic created from broken tile shards. Antoni Gaudí was the first to use this technique. He covered his three-dimensional architecture with ceramics of different shapes, reliefs and colours which create brightly colored patterns dancing together under the Mediterranean light.

The Güell Palace has 8 levels, from basement to roof terrace. It has a billiard room, an sculpture studio, a smoking room, a dressing room, a musicians' area, and many halls and bedrooms •

My advice

This is really an impressive building that reflects the immense wealth of the catalan bourgeoises at the turn of last century. The house is like a museum, well worth seeing.

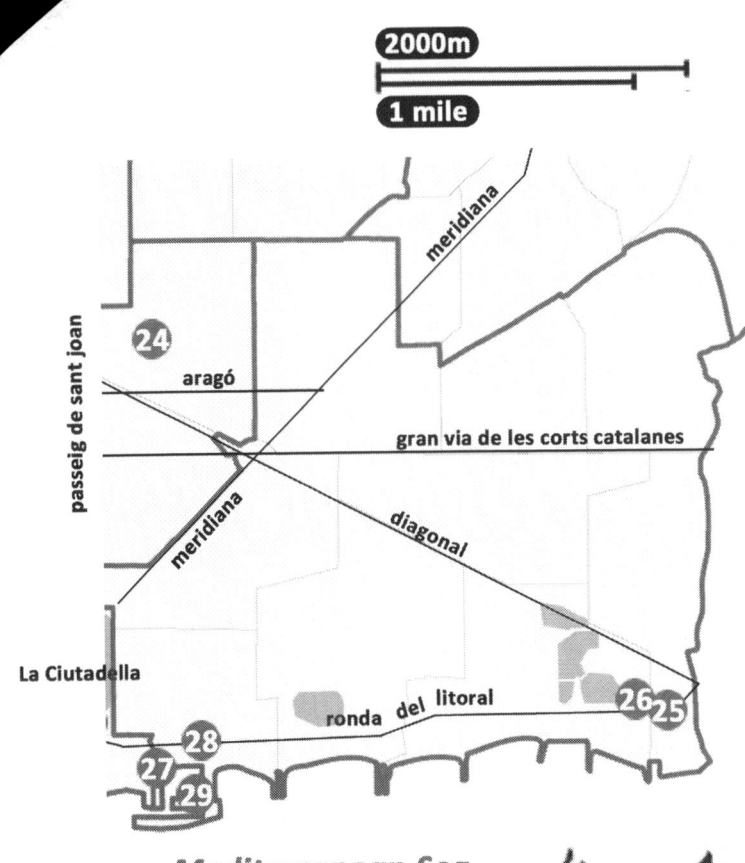

2000m

1 mile

meridiana

passeig de sant joan

24

aragó

gran via de les corts catalanes

meridiana

diagonal

La Ciutadella

ronda del litoral

26 25

28

27
29

Mediterranean Sea

N W S E

- Places
- 🚆 Stations
- Parcs
- **abcd** - Tourist info

Zone East

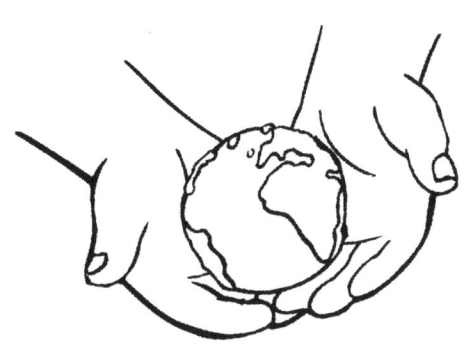

LA SAGRADA FAMILIA

Is it a cathedral? really?

at LA SAGRADA FAMÍLIA

pronounced "lah sah-gra-dah fah-me-lee-ah"

An impressive exterior with an incredible interior.
A forest of columns, bell towers and rosettes.

La Sagrada Família is probably Barcelona's most famous and most controversial work of Gaudí. Commenced in 1882, the ambitious young architect started building the church when he was only 31, during the last years of his life he even slept in the crypt. In his vision the Sagrada Familia should become a memorial of remorse for modern materialism in Barcelona: 18 majestic towers shall be crowned by another one in the centre with a total height of 170 metres. When concluded, this would be the highest building in Barcelona •

La Sagrada Família
Mallorca, 401
08013 BARCELONA - Tel. +34 935 132 060

L2-Sagrada Família, L5-Sagrada Família

10,19,33,34,43,44,50,51,V21,Bus Turístic

9am-8pm Mon to Sun (April to September and until 6pm the rest of the year). Morning only on 25-26/Dec, 1/Jan and 6/Jan.

www.sagradafamilia.cat

Zone EAST

Lat: 41.40323
Long: 2.17402

wanna go there

Betcha didn't know that...

Gaudí knew that his vision was too gigantic to conclude it during his lifetime. Until his death in Barcelona in 1926 (he was killed by a tram), he finished the crypt, one of the towers and most of the Christmas facade. Since then several architects and sculptors have contributed to the fulfilment of Gaudí's vision. Constantly under controversial discussion Barcelona's Sagrada Família shall be finished by 2030 – if there is enough financial support.

The construction of La Sagrada Família is not supported by any government or official church sources. Private patrons funded the initial stages. Money from tickets purchased by tourists and private donations are now used to pay for the work. The construction budget for 2009 was €18 million •

My advice

Very busy most of the year, arguably the busiest attraction in town. If you're visiting with children ensure you pre-book online to avoid the long queues. Worth visiting, although sometimes a few pictures from the outside just will do!

Zip wires, hanging platforms...

at the BOSC URBÀ

pronounced "bohsk oor-bah"

A new concept in adventure... conveniently located 'in' the city and that you can reach by tube, how cool is that, uh?

There is no need to leave the city to enjoy sports and adventure: zip wires, hanging platforms, ropes, bungee jumping, suspension bridges and trunks on platforms are just some of the many attractions that await you in the different circuits at **Barcelona Bosc Urbà**, which are designed for both boys and girls and their families, and for those who are eager to **experience strong emotions**.

Three circuits are available: *orange* for under 8 y.o. –with 14 platforms at a height of 1'5m from the ground–, *blue* for itermediate level –with platforms at a height of 4m from the ground– and *red* for those who love strong emotions. This circuit has platforms that are 6m from the ground and ends in a zip wire of more than 120m •

Barcelona Bosc Urbà
Plaça del Fòrum, s/n
08019 BARCELONA - Tel. +34 931 173 426

🚇 L4-El Maresme-Fòrum
🚌 7,41,43,141,Bus Turístic (stop: Fòrum)
🚆 T4-Fòrum

In summer daily from 10am-3pm and 4pm-8pm. For the rest of the year check their website as they have a very mixed schedule.

barcelonaboscurba.com

Lat: 41.41049
Long: 2.22032

Zone EAST

wanna go there

Betcha didn't know that...

The technology for modern bungee cords was developed for parachuting tanks. Bungee cords are made with hundreds of long interwoven individual rubber strands, each about 1mm (1/32 of an inch) thick. They can be designed to handle weights as heavy as a multi-ton machine or as light as your backpack.

The first suspension bridge structures were not made of steel and stones structures like today, they were made of hanging vines which are found in South America, Africa and Asia. Many years ago people made suspension bridges by hanging cables made of twisted vines. They tied these cables to trees on either side of a canyon or river. The suspension bridges were important to people and still are because this enables people to cross rivers and canyons faster •

For your info

Barcelona Bosc Urba is run by CETIO, a company that manages many projects related to sport. The safety and quality of the circuits has been certified by CERES CONTROL which specialises in the certification of constructions and safety in this type of parks.

Learn amazing facts about Earth

at the MUSEU BLAU

pronounced "moo-seh-oo blah-oo"

Do you like Natural Sciences?... this is your place! Over 9000m² of knowledge for everybody in a fun set up.

Discover **Planet Life**, a thrilling walk by the history of the evolution of life on Earth, from its origins to today: the origin of life, sex and reproduction, behaviour, evolution, ecology and conservation.

But, what will I find?... a whale skeleton, a gazillion fossils, stuffed animals (no, not the teddy bear type!), birds and fish of the past, stones and precious minerals, fantastic documentaries... what else do you want?. Get to know how we got to know what we know today! •

Museu Blau
Plaça Leonardo da Vinci, 4-5 – Parc del Fòrum
08019 BARCELONA - Tel. +34 932 566 002

L4-El Maresme-Fòrum

7,41,43,141,Bus Turístic (stop: Fòrum)

T4-Fòrum

10am-7pm Tue to Fri (8pm Sat and Sun).
In summer (June to September) is open until 9pm.

free

Zone EAST

Lat: 41.41160
Long: 2.22082

www.museuciencies.bcn.cat

wanna go there

Betcha didn't know that...

The Museu Blau is part of the Natural Science Museum Complex which is distributed across the city: Museu Martorell –explaining the history of science- and Laboratori de Natura – housing geology and zoology and a lab for experimenting- in Parc de la Ciutadella, and Jardí Botànic -14 hectares of plants, trees and flowers from all corners of the World (see #30)- in Montjuïc.

Many people in classical Greece believed that at the beginning of time there was only one being, which they called Chaos. Out of Chaos then came the earth (*Gaia*) and the sky (*Ouranos*). The Greeks thought of the earth as a woman and the sky as a man, because seeds go in the earth and yet it takes both the sky (the rain and the sun) and the earth to grow a crop •

My advice

For under 6 y.o. stop by the "Science Nest" at the 1st floor of the museum, they'll love it —open only on weekends. Also, if you are planning to visit the Botanical Garden —which, by the way, is in the other side of town!— do not forget to get a combined ticket (there's a bit of saving!)

Get lazy by the sea

at the ICÀRIA, BOGATELL and MAR BELLA

pronounced "ee-kah-reeah, booh-ga-tehl and mar beh-lee-ah"

#27

A perfect sunbathing spot that you can reach by metro or by bus, only a few minutes away... incredible!

Barcelona is an ancient city full of history, beautiful buildings, a zillion stores to buy anything you want, incredible attractions, and the best soccer team ever (well, I think so!)... and on top of all this it has two great natural resources that makes this city one of the best places in the whole world: **fantastic weather** and the **Mediterranean sea**.

And to take advantage of this you have over 6km of beaches to enjoy it... without ever leaving the city! The classical ones, **Sant Sebastià** and **La Barceloneta** (see #16) that have been used by Barcelonians since the beginning of times and the more modern **Icària**, **Bogatell** and **Mar Bella**, closer to the Olympic Harbour in the newest district of the city.

Ahh! what are vacations for if not for lazing around in the beach? ●

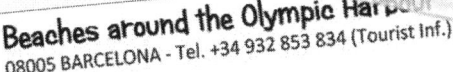

Beaches around the Olympic Harbour
08005 BARCELONA - Tel. +34 932 853 834 (Tourist Inf.)

L4-Ciutadella/Vil·la Olímpica
36,45,59,71,92,D20,V21,Bus Turístic

▶▶ free

Lat: 41.38628
Long: 2.19833

Zone EAST

Betcha didn't know that...

Most beaches in Barcelona are awarded the Blue Flag year after year. This is an international distinction that recognizes the beaches that meet appropriate conditions regarding the water quality, information security, accessibility or services.

Over 200 workers of the City's Cleaning Brigade -named BCNeta- clean the beaches every day so you can find them neat and tidy every morning. Help them by not littering!

Feel the urge of checking your email or chatting with your friends?, if you have an Internet-enabled device you can use one of the 14 free municipal wi-fi points located in the beaches. Look for a sign containing a white "W" on a blue background. Note though that browsing capabilities are quite restricted•

My advice

DO PAY ATTENTION to the flags waving in the beaches. "Green" means you can safely take a swim, "yellow" means that you must be very careful —either because of strong sea currents, floating jellyfish...— and "red" means that is dangerous to enter the sea so the water is a no—go area that day, got it?

See blockbusters in English

at the CENTRE DE LA VIL·LA

pronounced "sen-tra dah lah veel-ah"

The latest blockbuster releases while you are on vacation in Barcelona, and in English? why not?

El Centre de la Vil·la is a mall centre with shops and restaurants and it's well known in Barcelona for being the biggest movie theatre in town showing non-dubbed **blockbusters** (*uh-oh... that's "English" for you and me!*)

But of course, it's more than a cinema: got some free time before the movie begins? perhaps feeling a bit hungry?... fancy a Mexican burrito? delicious Middle Eastern *durums* and *falafels*? a slice of mouth-watering pizza? or simply a hamburger and some fries?

Then, when movie time has arrived, head to the lower floor to **Yelmo Cineplex Cinemas**: 15 screens are waiting for you, some in 2D and 3D —a high-definition format that produces a better quality and more realistic movies. Don't forget your popcorn! •

Yelmo Cineplex - Icària 3D
Salvador Espriu, 61 / Av. Icària, 154-166
08005 BARCELONA - Tel. 902 220 922 (local number)

M L4-Ciutadella/Vil·la Olímpica

14,36,41,71,92

www.yelmocines.es

Cinema: check schedules.
Mall (shops): from 10am–10pm Mon to Sat.

Lat: 41.39042
Long: 2.19860

Zone EAST

wanna go there

• •
Betcha didn't know that...

Movies at Yelmo cinemas are not dubbed, they are mostly in English, and with subtitles in Catalan or in Spanish. Many Thurdays in the evening you can also watch famous operas in high definition and with a superb sound system.

In cinemas over here, popcorn and light snacking is permitted during the show but, contrary to some theatres in the US, eating –as in a hamburger, pizza or nachos for example- is not •
• •

My advice

If you're planning to go to Yelmo Cineplex on a late night session note that public transportation in the area is quite reduced after 11.00pm. Did you miss the last bus or metro?... call a taxi (see section: "Useful tips" in page 209)

29

Sail in your very own private boat
at the OLYMPIC HARBOUR

Sailing your way around the city. Ahhhh, this one is a real treat! the ultimate experience while on vacation.

Sail in your own boat, like a superstar... relax while sunbathing and feel the sea breeze. Bring swimsuit and towel if you want, to swim if conditions permit.

Or become a true sailor, one of the crew, help trimming the sails and taking the helm as you navigate your way past beautiful beaches and experience the life at sea like an explorer or an adventurer. No previous sailing experience is required, as on board is a highly-experienced skipper to show you the ropes. A fun, safe and exciting way to enjoy Barcelona's magnificent skyline.

There are different companies offering this unique experience. Picture yourself getting into a beautiful sunset while enjoying a quiet sailing as well as an unusual image of the city. Are you going to miss this? •

Boating
Terms and expressions

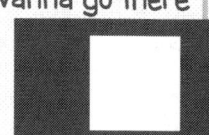

wanna go there

ABAFT = Toward the rear of the boat

BATTEN DOWN = Secure hatches and loose objects both within the hull and on deck. Particularly relevant when preparing for bad conditions

CAPSIZE = To turn over

COMPANIONWAY = The main entrance into the interior of the boat

DOCK = An area in which vessels are moored

DRAFT = The depth of water a boat draws

FENDER = A cushion, placed between boats, or between a boat and a pier, to prevent damage

FOULED = Any piece of equipment that is jammed or entangled, or dirtied

GALE = Storm with wind speeds of 34-40 knots

GYBE = Changing the direction of the boat by turning the stern of the boat through the wind

HALYARD = A line used to hoist a sail, the tightness of which effects the shape of the sail

HEAD = A marine toilet

HELM = The wheel or tiller controlling the rudder

JACOBS LADDER = A rope ladder, lowered from the deck, as when passengers come aboard

KEEL = The centreline of a boat running fore and aft; the backbone of a vessel

KNOT = A measure of speed equal to one nautical mile (6076 feet) per hour

LAZY JACK = A line running from the mast to the boom to aid lowering of the sail

LEE = The side sheltered from the wind

LOG = A record of courses or operation

MOORING = An arrangement for securing a boat to a mooring buoy or a pier

RIGGING = Lines, halyards or other items used to attach sails.

SCREW = A boat's propeller

SEAWORTHY = A boat or a boat's gear able to meet sea conditions

SPINNAKER = A large, light sail used when the wind is coming from behind the boat.

STEM = The forward most part of the bow

STOW = To put an item in its proper place

TILLER = A bar or handle for turning a boat's rudder or an outboard motor

TRIM = Fore and aft balance of a boat

VEER = Change of wind direction

YAW = To swing or steer off course

• •

YATESBCN
www.yatesbcn.com
tel. +34 669 299 727

SON A MAR
www.sonamar.net
tel. +34 617 366 362

VIAJES EN VELERO
www.viajesenvelero.es
tel. +34 607 240 600

These are an "on-request" attractions, not regularly scheduled ones, therefore booking is absolutely necessary and must be done at least 1 week in advance • The activity is subject to weather • 2 to 6 people • Departures in the morning, afternoon or evening • Duration: around 3h, full day excursions also available • Prices from 35€/person • Includes: skipper, insurance and fuel • Children under 18 years must be accompanied by an adult

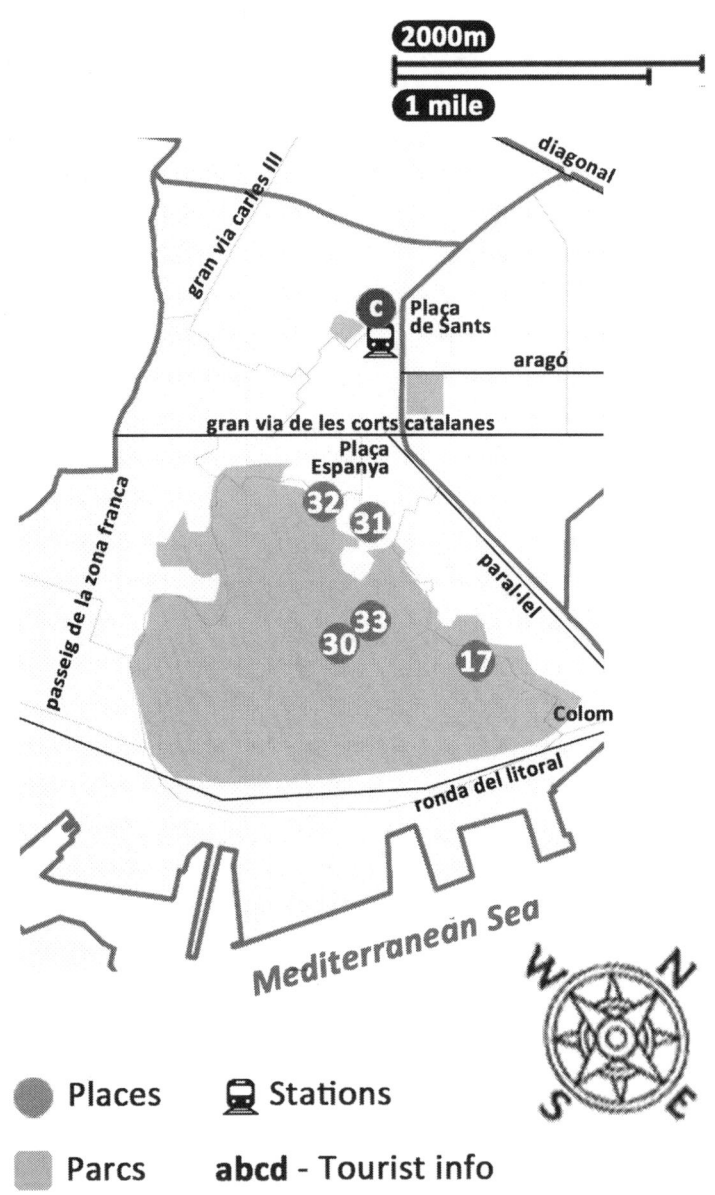

Places · 🚆 **Stations**

Parcs · **abcd** - Tourist info

Zone West

See flowers and curious plants

at the JARDÍ BOTÀNIC

pronounced "jar-dee boo-tah-neek"

Plants and trees from many countries around the World together in one super-garden. Ready for this, Indy?

The **Jardí Botànic** is located in the Montjuïc Hill –or 'mountain' like locals call it!- on a steeply sloping plot (140m above sea level at its highest point and 100m at its lowest) with splendid views of the city.

The gardens specialize in plants and communities from those areas of the world with Mediterranean climates and is divided into areas representing the main areas: the Mediterranean basin, Australia, Chile, California and South Africa. A specific section is devoted to the flora of the Canary Islands with a wide variety of pines, palms and dragon trees ●

Jardí Botànic
Doctor Font i Quer, 2
08038 BARCELONA - Tel. +34 932 564 160

L1,L3 and L8-Espanya + 30' walk uphill
13,55,150,Bus Turístic + 10' walk

10am to 8pm Mon to Sun in summer (June to August), to 7pm in April, May and Sept and to 6pm the rest of the year.

Lat: 41.36297
Long: 2.15771

Zone WEST

www.jardibotanic.bcn.es

Look for a wooden boardwalk crossing a small pond... try to spot there the beautiful dragon flies hoovering above the water. they are not very big so look carefully.

Betcha didn't know that...

The Jardí Botànic offers over 1500 species of plants and trees on display occupying a total area of 14 hectares, equivalent to 20 football fields.

Unlike other museums with collections of non-living materials, the Gardens are a constantly evolving, dynamic space. New species are grown every year in the nurseries and planted out in the grounds. The ones that fail to adapt to the climate or soil characteristics are removed from the collection •

My advice

Ideal to relax on a Sunday afternoon. If the weather is nice you should take a walk up from Plaça Espanya to the Botanic Garden, but if you're going with under-8s... take a bus to the gardens then, to return, just walk your way downhill to Plaça Espanya.

Sound, lights and music... action!

at LA FONT MÀGICA DE MONTJUÏC
pronounced "lah font mah-gee-kah dah mon-joo-eek"

An unmissable musical show featuring water fountains and coloured lights. A fairy tale spectacle!

Head down to the Montjuïc area and watch **La Font Màgica** (*The Magic Fountain*) a spectacular display of music, water acrobatics and lights which generate over 50 kinds of shades and hues.

La Font Màgica has become one of Barcelona's most popular attractions and is where the "**Piromusical**" is held every year at the end of September, a true balletic spectacle of water and light. A *pyromusical* is a huge fireworks display with a music, water and laser show, which is the closing event for Barcelona's main festival, **La Mercè** •

Font Màgica de Montjuïc

Plaça de Carles Buïgas, 1
08004 BARCELONA - Tel. +34 932 853 834 (Tourist Inf.)

 L1-Espanya, L3-Espanya, L8-Espanya (FGC)

 9,13,23,37,46,50,65,79,91,109,165,D20,H12

9pm to 11.30pm Thu to Sun in summer (May to Sept). 7pm to 9pm
Fri and Sat the rest of the year except during maintenance periods.
Sessions every 30'.

▶▶ free

bcn.cat/parcsijardins/fonts

Zone WEST

Lat: 41.37145
Long: 2.15223

The best spot is next to the big two towers, you'll be able to frame the fountain itself and the magnificent Palau Nacional as a background.

Betcha didn't know that...

The plant has a total of 3620 water jets and the largest diameter of the water basin is 35 meters. Five pumps ensure that 2600 litres per second of water run through a total of 1500 meters of pipelines to the jets.

The maximum water pressure corresponds to a column of a height of 54 meters. The fountains are controlled by 134 engines and 109 valves. The music comes from an impressive sound system and 6km of air pipes. Together with the lighting system of 8 different colours, it is cared for to put one into the mood.

Since a lot of water is pumped through this great fountain it'd be a waste of dr. It operates on recycled water in order to save drinking water •

My advice

The best time to see the fountain is at sunset... beware it gets a bit crowded in the summer months.

Cross the main gates and submerge yourself in a different era, when knights and peasants crowded the cities....

The **Poble Espanyol** contains 116 building in different architectural styles from the past 1000 years representing Spain's many regions. The village features a large square, the **Plaça Major**, and a couple of smaller squares connected by picturesque streets. It also has a town hall, a church, a monastery, shops and residential buildings.

There are also several replicas of famous Spanish monuments such as the Puerta San Vicente, one of nine gates of the 11th century walls around the city of Avila. Many buildings showcase Catalan and Spanish **artisanry** and several more function as charming cafes and restaurants. Sometimes there are also concerts in the main square •

Poble Espanyol

Avinguda Francesc Ferrer i Guàrdia, 13
08038 BARCELONA - Tel. +34 935 086 300

L1,L3 and L8-Espanya + 10' walk.
13,23,150,Bus Turístic (stops: Poble Espanyol)

9am to 8pm on mon. and until past midnight the rest of the week and on week-ends.

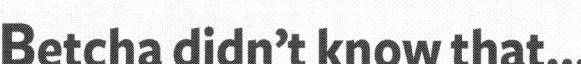

Zone WEST Lat: 41.36953 Long: 2.14718

www.poble-espanyol.com

There are plenty of beautiful spots: an Andalusian patio, a Galician Pazo, a Basc caserio, a Catalan masia... Make sure you've got a spare memory card.

Betcha didn't know that...

The original plan was to build the village as a temporary exhibition and demolish it after the world expo. However, the village become such a success during the world expo and proved so popular amongst the people that the village was allowed to remain.

The Poble Espanyol offers as well many activities for kids, such as the "Treasure Hunt", a gymkhana activity for families.

During the Spanish Civil War of the late 1930s and until the mid 40s, the village ceased to receive visitors and instead faced the cruel reality of the war and post-war occupation. Unknown to many is that the village was used as an interment centre for the nearby Castell de Montjuïc, which at the time was used as a prison ●

My advice

It can be a little bit touristy but it's also really beautiful. Good to combine Poble Espanyol with other things on Montjuic mountain. Don't forget to check their Art and Craft Shopping Center, if only to have a peek, it's worthwhile! Snacking is all right but avoid lunching or dinning there as restaurants are a bit overpriced and, to me, quality—price—service is not balanced.

Feel sporty

at the OLYMPIC STADIUM AND MUSEUM

33

Jump, run, kick, ride, dribble, stretch, spin, hit, throw... aren't you tired already?

Barcelona held the **25th Olympic Games** in 1992, but its 'olympic' past runs far back. Barcelona was the runner-up for the Games of 1936 which were finally celebrated in Berlin. **The Olympic Stadium** was built for this occasion. It has housed since several local sport teams, like the Barcelona Dragons –Barcelona's very own American football team- or RCD Espanyol (football) and during its 80 years of history has celebrated many events: the Mediterranean Games, the IAAF World Cup, the World Bowl V, the World Police and Fire Games, the European Athletics Championships... and also many concerts: Rolling Stones, Prince, Madonna, Michael Jackson, Bruce Springsteen, Coldplay, Prodigy or Shakira among others ●

Museu Olímpic i de l'Esport de Barcelona
Avinguda de l'Estadi, 60
08038 BARCELONA - Tel. +34 932 925 379

 L1,L3 and L8-Espanya + 20' walk uphill

55,150, Bus Turístic (stop: Anella Olímpica)

10am–8pm Tue to Sat, to 2.30pm on Sun and closed on Mon.
From October to March it closes at 6pm instead.
The Stadium is at Passeig Olímpic 17-19.

Zone WEST

Lat: 41.36650
Long: 2.15721

www.museuolimpicbcn.cat

wanna go there

Betcha didn't know that...

The Olympic Museum, next to the stadium, is a very high-tech installation with entertaining and educational shows that offer an overview of the sport in all disciplines and modalities. You'll even find a real F1 car and a tuned-up rally car!

The stadium has a capacity of 55,926 (67,007 during the 1992 Olympics), small if compared to the FC Barcelona "Camp Nou" which seats 100,000!

In 2001, the stadium was renamed after the former president of Catalonia, Lluís Companys, who was assassinated at the nearby Montjuïc Castle in 1940 by the dictatorial Franco regime •

The best shot at the Olympic Stadium is at the main entrance. there's a balcony overseeing the stadium.

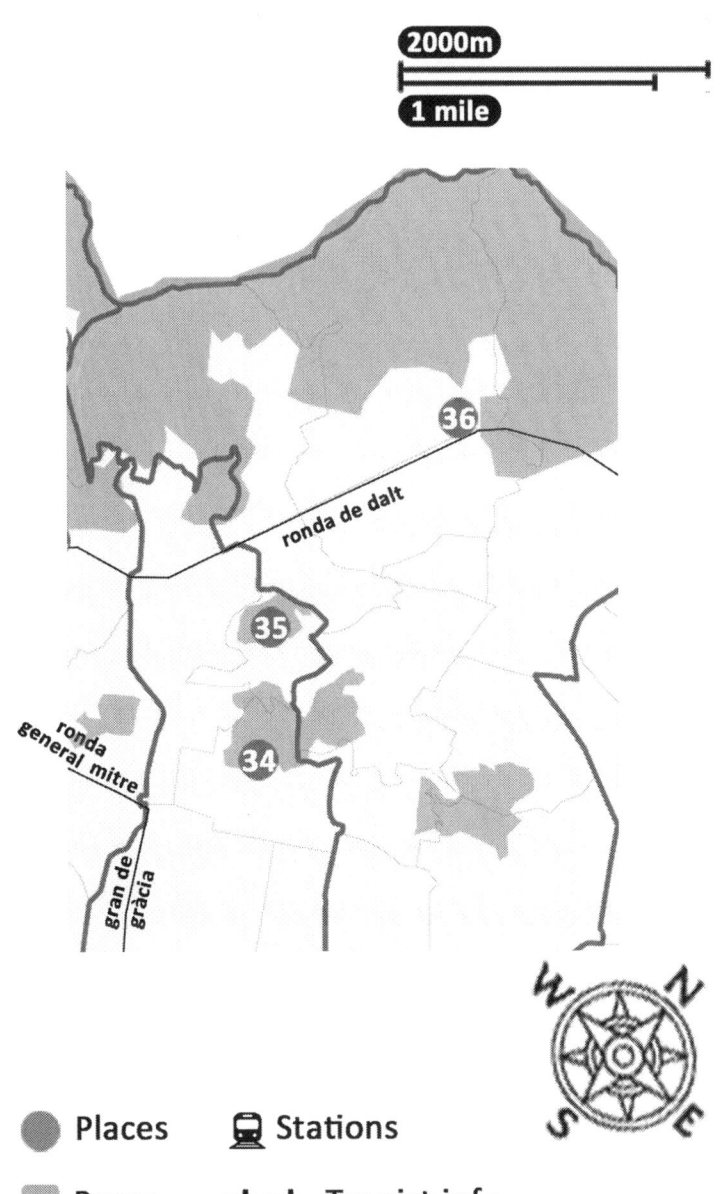

2000m

1 mile

ronda de dalt

36

35

ronda general mitre

34

gran de gràcia

● Places   🚆 Stations

▪ Parcs   **abcd** - Tourist info

Zone North East

Park Güell

A forest with magic monuments

at the PARC GÜELL

pronounced "park goo-ehl"

The most 'magical' park in Barcelona: surreal, almost cartoon-like constructions in a magnificent surrounding.

The **Parc Güell** was designed by architect Antoni Gaudí and built between 1900 and 1914 on the order of Count Güell as part of a housing site. However, the venture was commercially unsuccessful and, in 1922, Count Güell decided to give the land to the city on the condition that it was to be a public park forever so the citizens of Barcelona could enjoy it for generations to come.

Gaudí's characteristic vivid imagination is revealed in the different elements that amaze visitors of Parc Güell. At the main entrance, the flight of steps, with its famous dragon covered in coloured broken-ceramic pieces, leads to the hypostyle hall, an impressive space comprising 86 columns. For the younger there's the **Gaudí Experience**, a 3D show to introduce them to the world of Gaudí •

Parc Güell

Olot, 5-13

08024 BARCELONA - Tel. +34 932 853 834 (Tourist Inf.)

 L3-Vallcarca + 15' walk.

24,92, Bus Turístic (stop: Parc Güell)

www.parkguell.cat

From 8am to 9pm (spring/summer) and 8:30am to 6pm (rest of the year). Opens daily. Free for under 6 y.o. Access is limited to 800 visitors/hour. Advance purchase is strongly recommended.

 free €€

Zone NORTHEAST   Lat: 41.41382 Long: 2.15320

There two most popular spots are: by the dragon (or salamander) sculpture at the main entrance and at the main plaza, overlooking the Barcelona skyline.

Betcha didn't know that...

The Parc Güell was declared in 1969 a Historical-Artistic Monument of National Interest and then reinforced in 1984 when it was declared a World Heritage Site by UNESCO.

The Sala Hipòstila, which was supposed to house the garden city's market, is formed by 86 Doric columns. It has an excellent acoustics and you'll often find street performers playing there. It's also a good spot to cool down a bit since the temperature there is much lower than the rest of the park.

The unique shape of the serpentine bench enables the people sitting on it to converse privately, although the square is large. The bench is tiled and in order to dry up quickly after it rains, and to stop people from sitting in the wet part of the bench, small bumps were installed by Gaudí •

My advice

Things to visit: the dragon and stairs at the main entrance, the Sala Hipostola, the main plaza known as Nature square, the rose garden, the Planter's viaduct, the weird Carob's viaduct, the museum —which used to be Gaudi's home— and the Turo de les Tres Creus, the highest point in the park with an excellent view of the city.

Splash in the pond

at the PARC DE LA CREUETA
pronounced "park the lah crah-oo-eh-tah dahl cohl"

In the middle of this park you'll bump into a massive claw
... not that any giant robot left it there!

The **Creueta del Coll** is a sheltered park, with a large pond and a small island with palm trees –no coconuts though! In the summer the lake is transformed into a public swimming pool. It's a very shallow pool, no deeper than 60cm (2 feet), so ideal for the little ones. Yes I know, not very deep for real swimmers... yet you'll be able to splash around all you want.

Higher up, there is a second smaller pond with one of the most important elements of this park, a colossal 50 tons sculpture by *Eduardo Chillida*. The sculpture, named the **Elogi de l'Aigua** (In Praise of Water) has the shape of a massive claw and is suspended over the water by four steel cables giving it the illusion to be magically 'floating in the air'. Don't worry though, it won't fall! •

Parc de la Creueta del Coll
Passeig de la Mare de Déu del Coll, 77
08024 BARCELONA - Tel. +34 932 853 834 (Tourist Inf.)

L5-El Coll/La Teixonera + 10' walk

28,87,92,129

From 10am to dusk, daily. More info at "Green areas" at
www.bcn.cat/parcsijardins

www.bcn.cat/parcsijardins

Lat: 41.41837
Long: 2.14786

Zone NORTHEAST

wanna go there

Betcha didn't know that...

The lake is 2100 m² and albeit being very shallow, during summer months there are lifeguards watching what's going on both inside and around the pool, so parents can also relax a bit!

The park is 1.68 hectares –the size of 3 football fields- and originally the site was a quarry to obtain granite to make concrete for the buildings of the city.

The park is fully equipped: dressing facilities –to get changed-, a first aid post -in case someone gets hurt- and toilets for... well, you know! •

My advice

Given that Parc Guell is in the same area you might want to combine both visits: a healthy walk in Parc Guell admiring Gaudi's genius and then, at the back entrance take bus 28 direction Plaça Catalunya, three stops and you're ready for a splash in the lake at the Creueta del Coll. Don't forget your swimming costume/trunks!

36

Can you find your way out?

at the LABERINT D'HORTA

pronounced "lah-bah-reen door-tah"

Let's see who can find the fastest way to the centre of the maze... ready, set, go!

This is the oldest and most beautiful park in Barcelona. It was created at the end of the 1700s -just after the French Revolution- and it belonged to the Desvalls family, a very rich aristocratic family that donated it to the city in 1967.

The park consists of several areas: the **Boxwood** gardens, the **Domèstic** -which has a planting of camellias-, the **Jardí de Molses** (*the mosses*), the **Petit Laberint**, the **Romàntic** -with a small cascade and a channel ending in the 'Island of Love'- and, of course, the **Laberint** (*the maze*) located at the centre of the park. The Laberint is a 750 meter (820-yard) long maze created from pollarded cypress trees that gives name to the park. In the centre of the labyrinth is a statue of Eros, the god of love •

Parc del Laberint d'Horta
Passeig dels Castanyers, 1
08035 BARCELONA - Tel. +34 932 853 834 (Tourist Inf.)

L3-Mundet
27,60,73,76

From 10am to dusk, daily. More info at "Green areas" at
www.bcn.cat/parcsijardins

free

Zone NORTHEAST   Lat: 41.43780
                      Long: 2.14809

Betcha didn't know that...

The park also contains the Desvall Palace, which currently hosts an institute for gardening education as well as a specialized library. Next to the palace is the Torre Sobirana, an ancient medieval watchtower.

The gardens hosted receptions for sovereigns of Spain on several occasions.

Also, it has been used to shoot a scene of the movie "*The Perfume*" by director Tom Tykwer.

The park is 9.10 hectares, about the size of 13 football fields, but the number of visitors at any given time is limited to 750 people in order to preserve the delicate environment and structures of the area •

My advice

This park is a green jewel of Barcelona and I recommend visiting it. The only drawback is that is a bit far from downtown. However, this park is easily accessible by public transport.

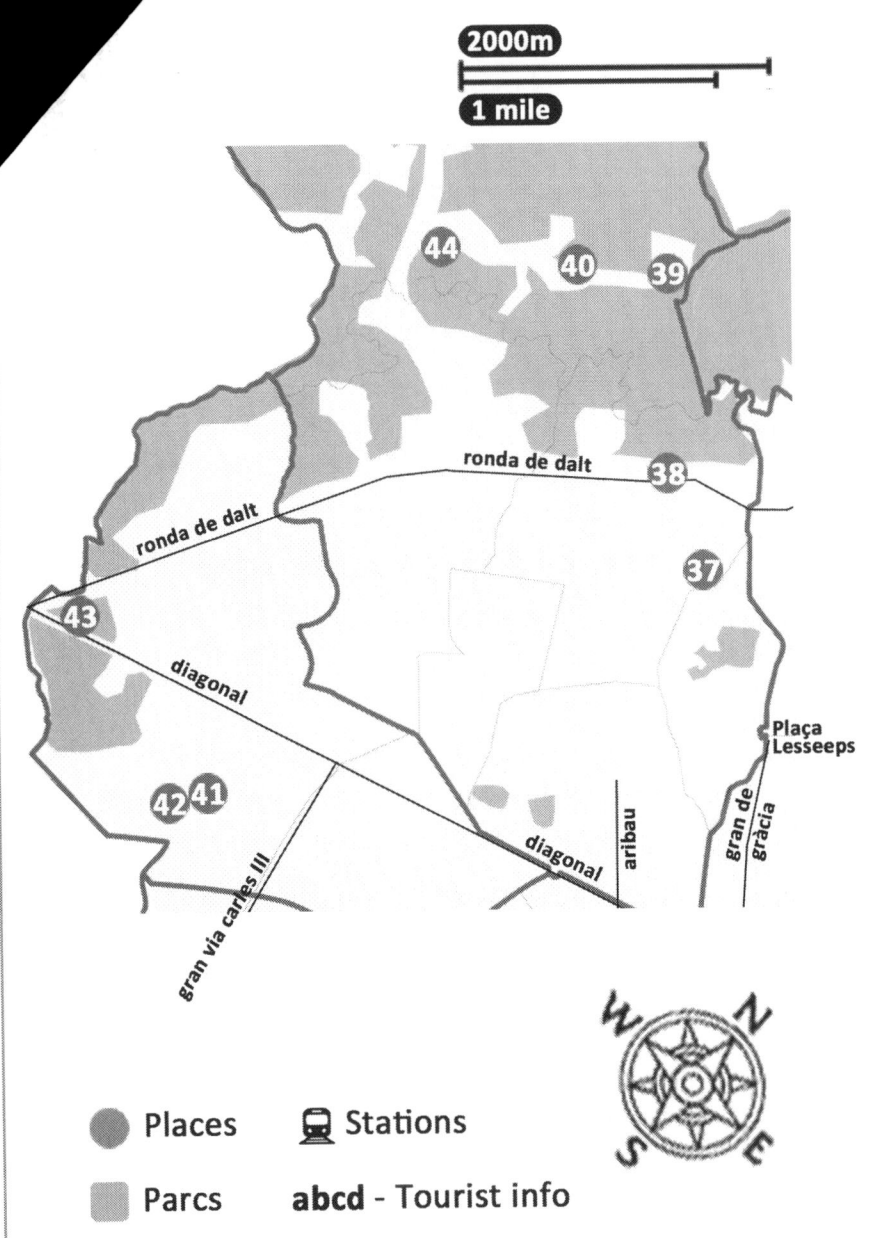

2000m

1 mile

ronda de dalt

ronda de dalt

diagonal

Plaça
Lesseeps

gran via carles III

diagonal

aribau

gran de gràcia

● Places   🚆 Stations

■ Parcs   **abcd** - Tourist info

Zone North West

Ride the oldest tram in town

#37

with the TRAMVIA BLAU (blue tram)

pronounced "tram-vee-ah blah-oo"

Slow but steady, climbing to the highest points
in Barcelona in the oldest tram in town.

Tramvia Blau (Catalan for "blue tramway") is one of Barcelona's three tram systems. It is a heritage streetcar line serving a hilly area north of the city between the terminus of metro L7 and the Funicular del Tibidabo. It was inaugurated in 1901. The old Barcelona tram lines were closed in 1971, but the Tramvia Blau route was kept open as a tourist attraction to show how transport was in the early twentieth century in Barcelona and because it is a nice way to get to the Tibidabo Fun Fair and Tibidabo hill. The final stop is at Plaça (*plah-sah*) Doctor Andreu where you can take the funicular up to the fair grounds or simply have a refreshment in a terrace of one of the bars while admiring the views of Barcelona from the tallest point in the city •

Tramvia Blau
Avinguda del Tibidabo, 2
08022 BARCELONA - Tel. +34 932 853 834 (Tourist Inf.)

www.tmb.cat/en/tramvia-blau

M L7-Av Tibidabo (FGC)
17,22,58,73,75,126,131,196,Bus Turistic
R

10am to 7:30pm. daily from June 22nd to Sept 11th. week-ends all
year around and public holidays. Departs every 20'.

▶▶ €

Lat: 41.41051
Long: 2.13895

Zone NORTHWEST

wanna go there

Betcha didn't know that...

On the tram's journey up the mountain you will pass through Barcelona's most affluent residential area. Take in the leafy surroundings and sneak a peek at the houses of the city's rich and famous.

The Tramvia Blau covers a route of 1276 meters with a height of 93 meters. Can you imagine having to walk it?... what a slope!

Albeit keeping the popular name "el Tramvia Blau", this line is officially Bus 194. Although the name of the service is blue tram, you can sometimes also see a red tram on the route, which is tram number 129 ●

My advice

If you're planning to go to El Tibidabo Fun Fair —see page 106— this is an excellent complement to the whole experience. Unfortunately though the Tramvia Blau is not fare-integrated with the other public transportation networks of the metropolitan area therefore you'll have to purchase additional tickets once on board.

38

Touch everything, yes go ahead...

at the MUSEU DE LA CIÈNCIA

pronounced "moo-seh-oo the lah see-ehn-see-ah"

Yes, you can touch, in fact, you're required to do so in this museum. Fun is <u>not</u> optional here.

The **Museu de la Ciència** (CosmoCaixa) offers a host of activities and exhibitions. It's a very hands-on museum which allows for interaction with the visitors. It's very fun!

Highlights of exhibitions include the **Bosc Inundat** (*the Flooded Forest*), which recreates 1000m² of an Amazonian rainforest ecosystem and features real piranhas, and small crocodiles; the **Geological Wall**, which illustrates the world's different geological structures; and the **Room of Matter**, an enthralling journey through the evolution of matter and life on our planet, with experiments, real pieces and living beings

It is designed with the younger ones in mind and has areas, such as the **Click & Flash**, the **Touch, touch!**, and the **Bubble Planetarium** for families •

Museu de la Ciència – CosmoCaixa
Isaac Newton, 26
08022 BARCELONA - Tel. +34 932 126 050

 L7-Av Tibidabo (FGC) + Tramvia Blau or Bus 196

 17,60,73,123,126,196

10am to 8pm Tue to Sun and public holidays. Opens Mon during the Christmas and Easter holidays, and in summer.

 free

Zone NORTHWEST   Lat: 41.41329
Long: 2.13054

Betcha didn't know that...

The Bosc Inundat (*the Flooded Forest*) at CosmoCaixa display some of the most dangerous animals in the planet, such as poisonous frogs, snakes, flesh-eating ants, crocodiles, alligators and piranhas.

This museum has over 100 exhibits that will require you to either push or press a button, pull a lever, touch a surface, turn a knob, stand up, sit down, lay down... it's one of the most fun museums around.

There is also Planetarium with a 3D stereo projection system that will allow you to experience being completely surrounded by the images in 3D using stereoscopic glasses •

My advice

You will need plenty of time (plenty!) to go through everything. It actually reminds me of a fun park. When I visit it I have the most fun just going through all the experimental attractions, the atmosphere is exciting, one feels like a kid in science class! Plan to spend quite a bit of time here so it's ideal for a rainy day.

39

Enjoy over 25 thrilling rides
at EL TIBIDABO (fun fair)
pronounced "al tee-bee-dah-boo"

A fun fair on top of a mountain... the best views of Barcelona while riding the wildest attractions.

El Tibidabo has more than 25 thrilling rides such as the **Atalaya** -a lookout tower that takes you over 50m up in the air-, the **Miramiralls** –the famous hall of mirrors that will make you look funny- or the **Witches and Wizards Den** -visiting the world of witches and wizards on a journey that is full of surprises while riding on an overhead carriage.

Check also the **Sky Walk** where you'll find the old **Avió**, the **Automatons Hall**, the **Rio Grande** train and the **Pony Rodeo** while enjoying the best views of the city. And of course, for the more daring you can ride the **Diavolo**, the **Pirate Ship**, the **Hurakan** and the **Roller Coaster**... all will sure make your head spin and your tummy turn! •

wanna go there

Parc d'Atraccions Tibidabo
Plaça del Tibidabo, 3-4
08035 BARCELONA - Tel. +34 932 117 942

Being in the outskirts of the city, your best bet is
to take the **Tibibus** in Plaça Catalunya which will
take you directly to the Torre de Collserola. And
it's even better if you combine this with #40.

12am to 11pm Wed to Sun during summer months and
week-ends the rest of the year. Check their website for
up-to-date information.

www.tibidabo.cat

Zone NORTHWEST   Lat: 41.42174
                   Long: 2.11908

Betcha didn't know that...

El Tibidabo fun fair was inagurated in 1901, making it one of the oldest in the world, yet it keeps constantly renovating its rides and adding new ones to amuse and amaze its young audience. It is located on top of the Tibidabo Mount, northwest of the city and 512 meters above the sea level.

The funicular operates on a line 1152 metres long with grades of up to 25.7% and a vertical ascent of 278.3 metres. Midway towards the El Tibidabo you'll find a signal marking 324 metres above the sea level, the same height as the Tour Eiffel.

L'Atalaya, the lookout tower, takes you up a further 50m up in the air, raising riders to a total height of 551m above the sea, the absolute highest point you can be anywhere in Barcelona.

Among the most emblematic rides are El Avió (*the Plane*), opened in the 1920s; The Hall of Mirrors, installed in 1905, and which was one the first concave-convex mirrors attraction in Europe; The Witches and Wizards Den –originally known as the aerial railway, and The Automatons Hall, the oldest dating from 1880 and the most modern from 2005 •

My advice

Note that this is an 'old style' fun fair: compact
and with attractions geared towards the younger
ones. Don't expect to find the latest—rides—
in—the—market, for that check Port Aventura
instead (see page 133)

Looking down from the sky

at the MIRADOR DE COLLSEROLA

pronounced "mee-rah-door toh-rah cool-sah-ro-lah"

The *stairway* lift to heaven: a vertigo-inducing lift ride takes you to the observation deck on the 10th floor.

The Collserola Tower is a main communications hub for the Barcelona Metropolitan Area, much like the BT Tower in London, the CN Tower in Toronto or the Sky Tree in Tokyo. It's full of antennae, satellite dishes and microwave transmitters that allow telephone communications and radio and TV broadcasts.

The Tower has an observation deck (or '*mirador*' in Catalan) on platform 10 located at 115 meters above the Turó de la Vilana (560 meters above the sea level) making it the highest point in the city •

Torre de Collserola
Carretera de Vallvidrera al Tibidabo
08017 BARCELONA - Tel. +34 932 117 942

Being in the outskirts of the city, your best bet is to take the **Tibibus** in Plaça Catalunya which will take you directly to the Torre de Collserola. And it's even better if you combine this with #39.

12am to 2pm and 3.30pm to 8pm Wed to Sun from Aug 1st to Sep 15st. For the other periods during the year check their website.

torredecollserola.com

▶▶ ⓒ€

Zone NORTHWEST

Lat: 41.41736
Long: 2.11485

Betcha didn't know that...

The panoramic lift takes only 2 minutes and a half to take you up from the base of the tower to the observation deck located in the 10th level, 115 meters above.

The Collserola Tower was conceived in 1987 by famous English architect Sir Norman Foster. It took 2 years to build, it has a total weight of 3000 tonnes and the top antenna reaches 288.4m (946 ft).

A large number of cables keep the tower upright. When it's windy, these cables make a lot of noise, that's why neighbours of the tower nicknamed it *"the guitar"* •

My advice

Reaching the tower might be a bit cumbersome as it's located in a remote area in the outskirts of the city, but the view is worth it. Get a good camera with powerful lenses... and you'll be able to take impressive pictures. Also note that is worthwhile to combine this attraction with a visit to the El Tibidabo fun fair (see page 106)

Watch football at its best

at the CAMP NOU, home of Barça

pronounced "camp noh-oo"

The best football team in the world! You might disagree with me... but I'm the one writing this guide, ain't I? ;)

FC **Barcelona** –or Barça (pronounced "*bar-sah*")- was founded in 1899 by a group of Swiss, English and Catalan footballers, the club has become a symbol of Catalan culture and Catalanism, hence the motto "Més que un club" (*More than a club*). The club is widely known as the 'Blaugrana' in reference to the colours of the club shirt, scarlet and blue, in the Catalan language. The shirt's crest consists of the St. George Cross -patron of Catalonia- in the upper-left corner with the Catalan flag beside it, and the team colours at the bottom •

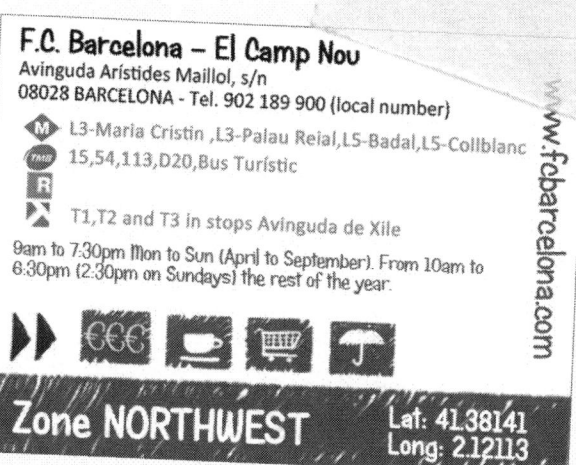

F.C. Barcelona – El Camp Nou
Avinguda Arístides Maillol, s/n
08028 BARCELONA - Tel. 902 189 900 (local number)

M L3-Maria Cristin ,L3-Palau Reial,L5-Badal,L5-Collblanc
TMB 15,54,113,D20,Bus Turístic
R
  T1,T2 and T3 in stops Avinguda de Xile

9am to 7:30pm Mon to Sun (April to September). From 10am to
6:30pm (2:30pm on Sundays) the rest of the year.

Zone NORTHWEST   Lat: 41.38141
                        Long: 2.12113

www.fcbarcelona.com

wanna go there

Betcha didn't know that...

It has won nearly 80 national and international trophies in its 112 years of history among which 3 European Cups and 4 Spanish League cups in the last 6 seasons alone!

Camp Nou is the largest stadium in Europe with a capacity of 99354 seats. It's impressive to look at the stands from the centre of the field. Why not come to a match?... and don't forget to get your season jersey with your name stamped on the back as a souvenir.

Barça also has professional sports teams in club competitions in basketball, roller hockey, handball, futsal, rugby, baseball, ice hockey, volleyball, athletics, figure skating, women's football and field hockey.

Unlike many other football clubs, the supporters own and operate Barcelona. It has over 176000 paying members and an annual turn-over of €398 million. In 2010, Forbes evaluated Barcelona's worth to be around €752 million (USD $1 billion) •

My advice

Nou Camp is a very popular attraction so expect queues, especially during summer months. Better if you book online in advance. The Club has created a packaged tour called "Camp Nou Experience" which includes a complete tour of the stadium, a visit to the museum and the multimedia area.

Ice skating all year round?

at the PISTA DE GEL DEL BARÇA

pronounced "peas-tah dah gel dahl bar-sa"

42

Looking for something new to try? what about ice skating in this hot weather? yes, I am not pulling your leg.

The **Pista de Gel del Barça** has hosted, among other events, important international ice hockey, figure skating and table tennis tournaments, as well as the world fencing championship. It has been also used to record several TV advertisements from well known brands.

It is an ideal space for all age groups to enjoy a day out for cool fun on ice skates, especially during the hot months of the year in Barcelona. If you are into ice hockey, figure skating or just a novice this is the place to come. A healthy activity for all ages and perfect for sharing with friends and family •

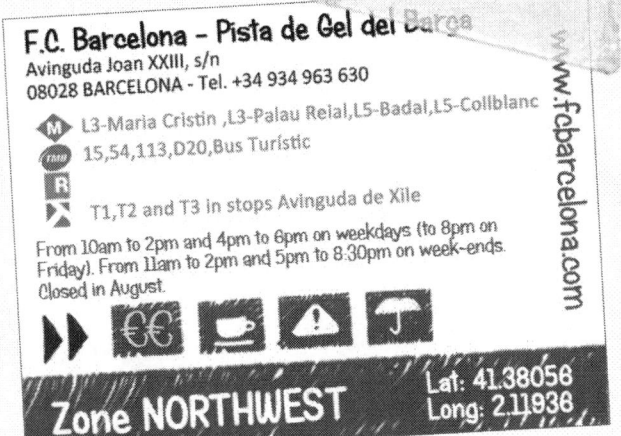

F.C. Barcelona – Pista de Gel del Barça
Avinguda Joan XXIII, s/n
08028 BARCELONA - Tel. +34 934 963 630

🅜 L3-Maria Cristin ,L3-Palau Reial,L5-Badal,L5-Collblanc

🚌 15,54,113,D20,Bus Turístic

🅡
🚊 T1,T2 and T3 in stops Avinguda de Xile

From 10am to 2pm and 4pm to 6pm on weekdays (to 8pm on Friday). From 11am to 2pm and 5pm to 8:30pm on week-ends. Closed in August.

www.fcbarcelona.com

Zone NORTHWEST Lat: 41.38056 Long: 2.11936

Betcha didn't know that...

The FC Barcelona complex includes, apart from the Camp Nou stadium, several other buildings among which an ice rink -called *Pista de Gel del Barça*- which is open all year, except for the month of August, in which is closed for maintenance. If you're vacationing in Barcelona in August, the Skating Club ice rink at Roger de Flor, 168 (tel. +34 932452800) is open.

The pavilion covers 3650m2 and the rink itself is 61 x 26 metres. It holds a capacity of 1256 spectators.

The Pista de Gel del Barça was opened in 1971, at the same time as the Palau Blaugrana —FC Barcelona's basketball arena— and it's home to two of the club sections: the ice hockey team and the figure skating team •

My advice

Minimum age admittance is 4 y.o. or from a size 26 foot. The use of gloves and socks is compulsory while skating. They can be bought there. Under—12s must also wear a helmet. This can be rented, alongside the skates, at the premises. Personal monitors are also available. Non—skaters don't have to pay anything.

Smell a beautiful rose garden

at the PARC DE CERVANTES

pronounced "park ser-van-tes"

A rose garden named
after the author of Don Quixote

The **Parc Cervantes** Rose Garden has around 10000 rosebushes of some 2000 species that, at the peak flowering period - between May and July - may produce **150000 roses blooming at a time**. It's an image of lush greenery and colour in a landscaped area covering some 9 hectares. The collection of roses are set out along an unusual botanical trail featuring varieties in all shapes and colours from every continent of the world. The area where roses bloom from April to November, due to Barcelona's mild climate, is known as the **Pèrgola**. Since 2001, the park has hosted an international rose show featuring new species which are added to its collection, which includes 245 different varieties •

Parc Cervantes
Avinguda Diagonal, 708-716
08034 BARCELONA - Tel. +34 932 853 834 (Tourist Inf.)

Ⓜ L3-Zona Universitària

🚍 7,33,54,60,67,75,113,H6

Ⓡ T1,T2 and T3-Zona Universitària + 5' walk

10am to 9pm daily (May to Sept). to 7–8pm in spring and autumn and to 6pm in winter. More info at "Green areas" at www.bcn.cat/parcsijardins.

▶▶

Zone NORTHWEST   Lat: 41.38349 Long: 2.10758

www.bcn.cat/parcsijardins

Betcha didn't know that...

The park has also a children's play area and a picnic area shaded by a pine forest, which is often used as a place to practice Tai-Chi. It is distinguished by its large expanses of grass, wide pathways and the gentleness of the slope of the land. No dogs allowed in this park!

Saint George's Day -patron of Catalonia- also known as The Day of the Rose is a Catalan holiday held on April 23th with similarities to Valentine's Day. The main event is the exchange of gifts between sweethearts. Historically, men gave women roses, and women gave men a book to celebrate the occasion —"a rose for love and a book forever." In modern times, the mutual exchange of books is also customary.

Roses have been associated with this day since medieval times and are valued for their romantic symbolism but their blooms are also edible. No, they don't taste like chicken. Rather like the flavours of green apples and strawberries ●

My advice

You might want to combine this activity with a visit to the Parc de Pedralbes, only 700m away, which is home to the Pedralbes Palace once the residence for the Spanish kings when visiting Barcelona. While the palace itself can't be visited, the gardens surrounding it are breathtaking.

Get adventurous on nature walks

at the PARC DE COLLSEROLA

pronounced "park dah cool-sah-ro-lah"

A park where you can run into a wild boar.
Honest! Cross my heart and hope to die.

The **Parc de Collserola**, with over 8000 hectares, is a true green island in the middle of one of the most densely populated urban areas on the Mediterranean coastline. The word "parc" can induce confusion here as this is not a regular park: no gates, no flower beds, no tree islands, no toilets, no facilities –other than the Information Centre-... but **a huge wild forest** instead with trails and itineraries for walking, hiking, bird watching, biking or jogging –but no camping or barbecuing! There are also many vantage points that allow for spectacular views of the whole city of Barcelona •

Parc de Collserola Information Centre
Carretera de l'Església, 92 / Carretera a Sant Cugat km 4.7
08017 BARCELONA - Tel. +34 932 803 552

 S1-Baixador de Vallvidrera (FCG) + 10' walk

The park is an open area not subject to schedules.
The Information Centre opens daily from 9:30am to 3pm
except on Dec 25th and 26th and Jan 1st and 6th.

▶▶ free

parcnaturalcollserola.cat

Zone NORTHWEST

Lat: 41.41916
Long: 2.10010

Betcha didn't know that...

Nearly 50% of the population of Catalonia lives less than ten kilometres away from the park, which makes in the largest metropolitan park in the world: 8 times larger than the Bois de Boulogne in Paris, and 22 times larger than Central Park in New York.

Some 300 species of animals can be found here: mammals like wild boars, genets, stone martens, badgers, rabbits and squirrels; birds like whitethroats, treecreepers, woodpeckers, bee eaters, doves, goshaw and sparrow hawks and also amphibians and reptiles: salamanders, newts, green tree frogs, the small southern frog, toads, small turtles, the ocellated lizard, snakes (nonpoisonous though!).

The Collserola mountain range has several historical sites among which the Iberian villages of Penya del Moro, puig Madrona and turó de Ca n'Oliver, all over 2550 years old. These were some of the first Barcelonians •

My advice

The closer to the city limits the odd house here and there and the more people you'll find, on Sunday mornings as it's very popular among Barcelonians. The Information Centre can provide maps with different recommended itineraries but remember: this is a wild forest.

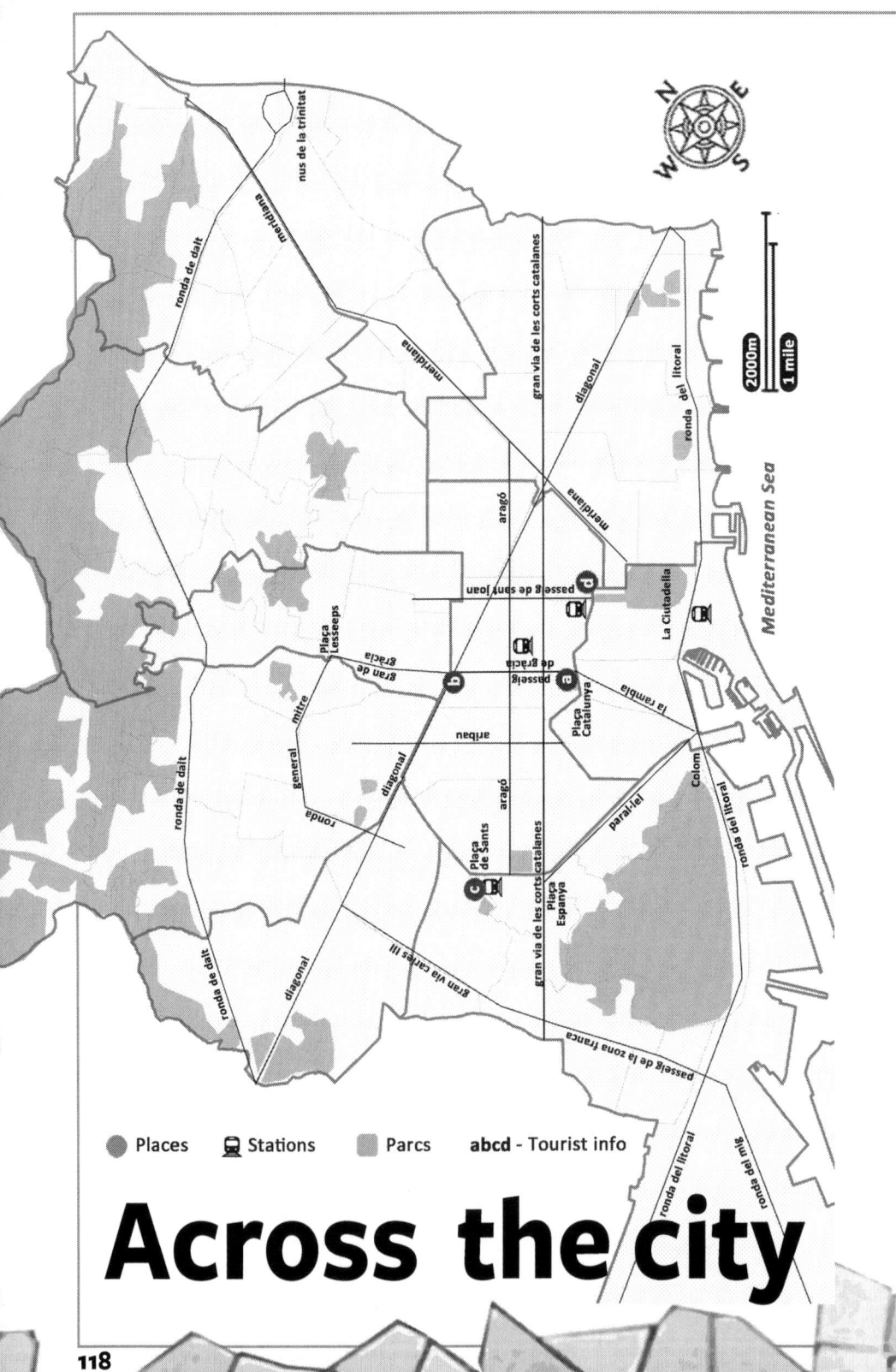

Places   Stations   Parcs   **abcd** - Tourist info

Across the city

Take a hop on hop off ride
with a tourist bus

45

Get to know Barcelona in the most comfortable way: a ride in an open roof double-decker.

Barcelona has two tourist bus companies, **Bus Turístic** and **Barcelona City Tour**. Both offer hop-on hop-off double-deckers to drive you through the city showing you the most well known spots without having to worry about the myriad of the public transport network stops, hubs or lines. Both companies operate open roof double-deckers as well, a nice touch given the pleasant weather in Barcelona and both depart from Plaça Catalunya. Bus Turístic –green and white buses- has three routes (blue, red and green) with 44 stops while Barcelona City Tour –red buses- has two routes (green/east and orange/west) with 34 stops. While on board they provide audio guides in many languages so you can know more about what you're seeing. Handy!

Barcelona City Tour

Tel. +34 933 176 454 (BCT Customer Service)

Daily service all year round (except Jan 1st and Dec 25th) • Journey time: 2.5 hours approx. for the East Route (green) and 2 hours for the West Route (orange) • Frequency: between 10' and 15' depending on the season.

9am to 8pm from Apr to Oct. and to 7pm rest of the year.

barcelonacitytour.cat

Zone ACROSS

Lat: 41.38704
Long: 2.18915

Bus Turistic

Tel. +34 932 853 834 (Tourist Information Office)

Daily service all year round (except Jan 1st and Dec 25th) • Green Route is open from March 30th to Nov 4th • Journey time: 2 hours per route except the Green Route, which takes 40 minutes • Frequency: between 5' and 25', depending on the season

9am to 8pm in summer. to 7pm in winter

barcelonabusturistic.cat

Zone ACROSS

Lat: 41.38614
Long: 2.18972

The Columbus statue, La Ciutadella, the seafront, FC Barcelona stadium, Plaça Catalunya, La Pedrera, Parc Güell, Montjuïc, Tibidabo... after all these you sure will know Barcelona as well as any local. And you can hop on and off where you want!

Of course there are other types of guided tours you can take in Barcelona: walking tours, tours on all type of bikes, gocar, segway, scooter, sidecar, roller skates, boat, limousine and even by helicopter. For more information check the next activity (#46) or phone +34 932 853 834 (Tourist Information)... but nothing is as convenient as the hop-on hop-off bus. Give it a try! •

Discover the city on your own time

#46

by bicycle, *sense presses!*

pronounced "sen-sah preh-sas" (it's Catalan... google for it!)

At your own pace and taking your time: by bicycle, tandem, segway, trike or by whatever you can think of!

Barcelona is a beautiful, romantic and kind-of-compact city. She's fairly flat (well, most of her!). Weather is normally very nice: hot and sunny in summer and mild and sunny in winter. She has a 186km long bike lane network. She also has parks and gardens all over, a cozy old city centre and a magnificent seafront promenade. Does this sound as the **perfect set for a bicycle tour** or what?

Barcelona has a large-scale public bike sharing system called "Bicing" (of course!). But the service is intended only for its residents. But don't worry, it is possible to hire bicycles -even with baby seats-, roller blades, tandem bikes, segways, go-carts and trikes from many rental bike shops spread across the city. And what about a guided city bicycle tour?

Segway...
www.segwaytours.cat
www.barcelonasegwayfun.com
www.segwaystp.cat

Classic sidecar
www.ridebrightside.com

Scotter...
www.via-vespa.com
www.tumotorent.com
www.barcelona-moto-rent.com

Helicopter...
www.barcelonahelicopters.com
www.cathelicopters.com

Go-car...
www.gocartours.com

Rickshaw...
www.trixi.com

Bike...
www.fattirebiketours.com
www.barcelonabybike.com
www.bicicletabarcelona.com
www.barcelonarentabike.com
www.bikerentalbarcelona.com
www.bajabikes.eu
www.budgetbikes.eu
www.bikinginbarcelona.net
www.greenbikesbarcelona.com
www.bornbikebarcelona.com
www.barcelonaturisme.cat

There are several specialised companies offering this service with guides from all sizes and shapes. Do you need an expert on medieval city architecture that can offer a tour in Japanese while riding a one-wheel bicycle?... no problem!

It's forbidden to lock bicycles to trees, traffic lights, benches and litter bins and if you do you risk having your bike removed by the police. There are the so-called 'anchor points for bicycles' spread across the city, these are silver painted U-shaped upside-down metal tubes for securing bicycles on the street. Use them, they are free! Also, do not leave your unlocked bike unattended, not even for a minute, as bike thieves operate in all districts of the city •

Touring the city on 8 wheels

with inline skates in a guided tour

did you think I meant 'by lorry', you silly?

47

The funniest way to visit the city, put on your skates and come to enjoy a crazy tour with a motley crew of skaters.

Every other <u>Saturday afternoon</u> the **Escola de Patinatge** (*The Inline Skating School*) organize tours for beginners so that all their students can improve their skating skills, safely on the street. But these tours are open to anyone willing to join. You can visit the city on 8 wheels in a very relaxed, casual and fun group. The length of the tour is open, you can join in or leave any time and anywhere you want. There are no preset routes and tours tend to be promenades by the seafront, the small streets in the city centre and the nearly flat Eixample district... in all looking for an easy time while discovering the city.

These tours are free for everybody. You have to know basic turns and how

My advice

You might not have a pair of skates with you —after all you are on vacation abroad!— but, no problem... you can rent them at www.inercia.com or at www.lockerbarcelona.com. It is strongly recommended to wear all the protections: knee and elbow pads and helmet. Kids must be accompanied by a parent during the tour.

where?

WWW.ESCOLAPATINATGE.COM
tel. +34 933 005 070 / 625 633 389

The meeting point is Passeig Garcia Fària at the corner of Josep Plà street in the far east side of the city. But these are directions to the meeting point, not to the school. The meeting time is normally on Saturdays at 5pm in winter and 6pm in summer. You do not need to call or make a reservation; just show up there and join the group. The organisers are identified with the word "col·laborador" on their T-shirts. Check the calendar at their website or phone to confirm the group will meet as there are some vacation periods during the year.

meeting point

Passeig Garcia Fària at the corner of Josep Plà street (close to Diagonal Mar Shopping Centre)

to stop with the heel brake (at least!) to participate safely. The School volunteers will help you and guide you throughout the tour. Sometimes up to 50 people get together. Can you imagine such a swarm skating on the streets of the city?. Don't think twice and join them, you'll have a great time! •

A walking tour learning about the city

with a professional tour guide

Learn about Barcelona with the best storytellers.
"... and to the left you will find a magnificent..."

Since 2,500 years ago, Barcelona has been... a commercial port for the Greeks, a Roman settlement, a frontier stronghold for Christianity, a vibrant Jewish community, capital-city of the Catalans since the birth of Catalonia, the centre of a maritime empire for over 300 years, home port for Columbus upon his return from America, a defeated city stripped off its power and heritage under the Bourbons in the 1700s, a reborn influential economic centre only 150 years later, a cornerstone of the Industrial Revolution in Europe, source of many entrepreneurs to the Americas in the 1800s, subjugated later in the 20th century by several Spanish dictators but 'freed' again in the 1970s, a

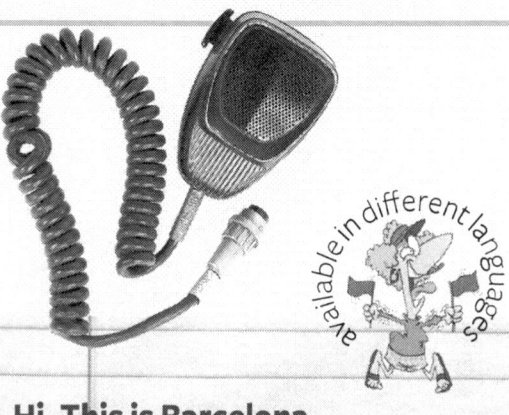

available in different languages

Hi. This is Barcelona..
www.hithisisbarcelona.com

Forever Barcelona
www.foreverbarcelona.com

Barcelona Tour Guides
www.barcelonatourguides.com

Pepito Tours
www.pepitotours.com

Barcelona Guide Bureau
www.bgb.es

Private Tours Barcelona
www.privatetoursbarcelona.com

My Favourite Things
www.myft.net

Toursbylocals.com
www.toursbylocals.com/barcelona-tours

Runner Bean Tours
www.runnerbeantours.com
(ask for their Kids&Family walking tour)

magnet for tourism in Europe, home of the Olympic Games in 1992, an influential city across the world in the 21st century... and of course, home to Barça. What a fascinating history!

But with so much to see and be learnt and so little time a guided walking tour is your best bet •

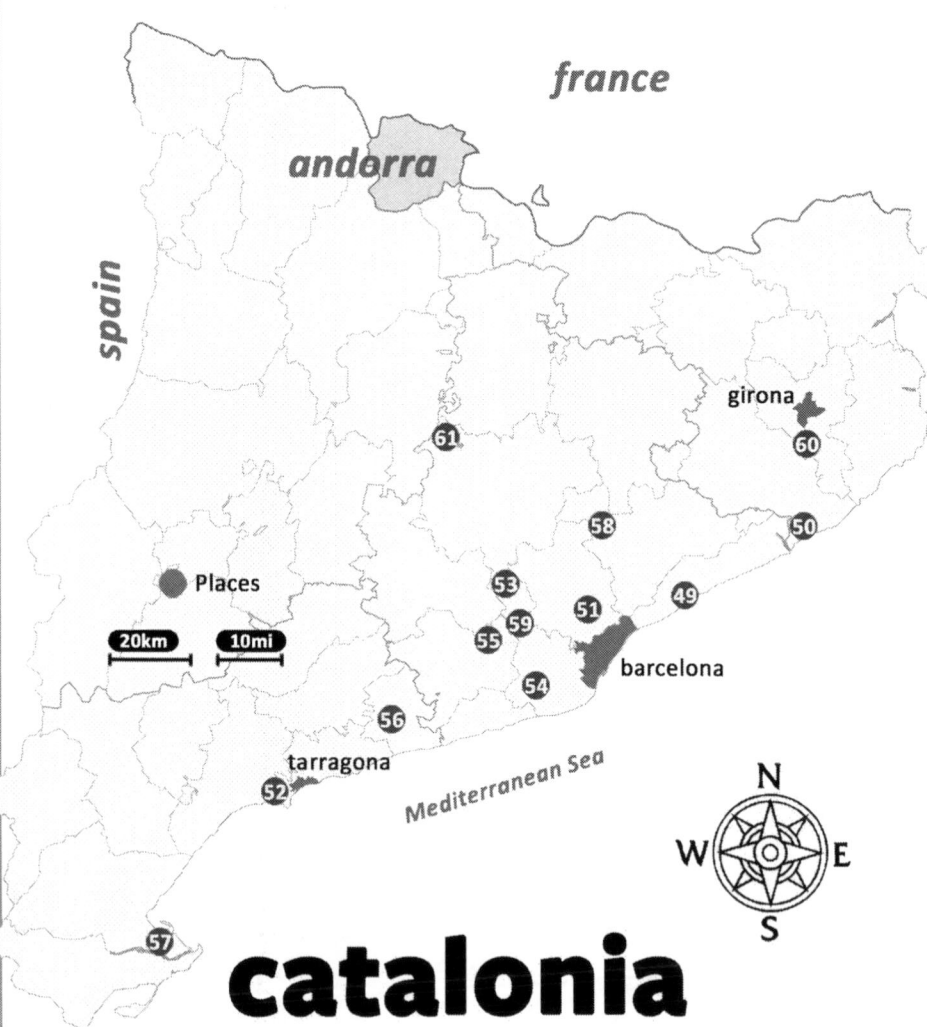

france

anderra

spain

girona

60

61

58

50

Places

53

59

51

49

20km   10mi

55

barcelona

54

56

57

tarragona

52

Mediterranean Sea

N

W   E

S

catalonia

Check the "Metro Network Map" on page 219
to locate the main train stations in Barcelona

Around the city

#49 A very fun waterpark
at ILLA FANTASIA in Vilassar de Dalt

pronounced "ee-lah fahn-tah-see-ah"

Ride the *Super Toboggan* -a smooth descent that allows you to enjoy the excitement of a 10 meter slide blinded by the emotions of the running water splashing all over your body until you end up into the pool- or take a chance with the *Kamikazes* –where screaming will not be of any help. Perhaps you prefer crossing the bridges and the water jets of the *Pirate Labyrinth*, going down the *Espirotub*, across the *Wild River,* at the *Waves Pool*... so many attractions... but they all guarantee you'll get completely soaked with fun! ●

My advice

It's obvious but... bring a swimsuit and a towel!... and plenty of sunscreen lotion of course. While not necessarily the best, this is the closest waterpark, and probably the most convenient, to Barcelona. Get a combined ticket which includes: entry to the park for one day, return trip to Premià de Mar and free shuttle bus to the waterpark. Buy it directly at the RODALIES station in Plaça Catalunya. Ask for a "combined ticket Illa Fantasia". Get off the train at Premià de Mar -about 25'-, cross the subway under the road and you'll see the bus stop for the shuttle. It operates every 15' and it takes 10' to reach the park. Check schedules though. Once in the parking lot at Illa Fantasia, look for the RENFE Exchange Booth and exchange your tickets to get into the park ●

www.illafantasia.com

Illa Fantasia
Finca Mas Brassó, s/n
08339 VILASSAR DE DALT
Tel. +34 937 514 553

Schedule: 10am to 7pm. Opens from Jun to mid Sep. Online ticket purchase cannot be done for the same day.

Getting there: From Plaça Catalunya (RODALIES) take line R1 -direction Mataró/Maçanet-Massanes- to Premia de Mar station then a free shuttle bus to the waterpark. Also possible to take a direct bus. Check their website.

FREE for under 90cm (3 feet) tall

Lat: 41.50305 ● Long: 2.38393

wanna go there

Raft like a pro

at WATER WORLD in Lloret de Mar

pronounced... well... "water world". what else?

Over 20 superb rides for all ages, from the calmed *Kiddie Island* to the furious *X-Treme Mountain*. From the wave pool to an endless slide at *Water Gegant*, the *Rafting River* – riding a round boat through dark tunnels while turning 360°-, the *Storm* –feeling sucked into the pool by a tremendous water force-, racing with your family at the *Water Pistes* -4 straight parallel slides-, who'll finish first? These and other rides will be waiting for you at **Water World Lloret**. No doubt one of the best waterparks, if not the best, in all the Mediterranean coast •

Water World Lloret
Ctra. Vidreres, km 1,2
17310 LLORET DE MAR
Tel. +34 972 368 613

Schedule: 10am to 6-7pm. Opens mid May to mid Sep. Tickets online available.

www.waterworld.es

Getting there: From El Clot-Aragó (RODALIES), take line R1 -direction Maçanet-Massanes- to Blanes station then a regular bus to Lloret bus station and then a shuttle bus to the waterpark.

Lat: 41.70858 • Long: 2.83032

My advice

Since it's a bit far from the city get an early start to seize the day and remember the very last train departs from Blanes a few minutes before 10pm, after that there are no more trains until the following day. Get a combined ticket which includes: entry to the park for one day, return trip to Blanes, bus to Lloret and shuttle bus to the waterpark. Buy it directly at the RODALIES station at El Clot-Arago, east of the city. Ask for a "combined ticket Water World Lloret". Get off the train at Blanes -around 75'- then take the bus to Lloret bus station -add some 15'- and then the shuttle to the water park -around 10'. From the bus station in Lloret to the park, the shuttle departs every 30 minutes, starting at 9am •

wanna go there

Tibetan bridges and more

at NATUPARK in Cerdanyola del Vallès

pronounced "nah-too-park" in Catalan!

Are you ready 007? Get your 'mission briefing', your safety tips and gear up. Head to the training circuit. Once you've got the grip on the ropes then you're ready to enter one of the other circuits: green, blue or orange for those under 1.45m tall (4 feet 9 in), red for taller kids and black for the dare devils. Up to 3 hours of pure adrenaline! And after the fun in the air, let's have a bite in the picnic area to recharge, then head to have fun in the water. A swimming pool is waiting for you at the nearby Bosc Tancat •

My advice

Minimum admittance age is 4 y.o. and 1 meter tall (3 feet 2 in). It's important to make a reservation to ensure the availability of equipment: harnesses, helmets... Over 10 instructors monitor the circuits to make sure you're safe. Some of the them do speak English. Children under 14 y.o. must be accompanied by an adult during the circuit (yes, that means mum or dad will have to participate too!) The park is certified as complying with the EU safety standards for adventure parks, so tell your parents to put their minds at rest. Bring your mosquito repellent... this is a forestry area •

www.natupark.com

NatuPark
Riu Sec, s/n -Pol. Ind Polizur
CERDANYOLA DEL VALLÈS
Tel. +34 935 910 727

Schedule: 10am to 6-7pm, Mon to Sun (in summer). The rest of the year the schedules vary depending on the season. Check their website. Important: book in advance!

Getting there: From Plaça Catalunya (RODALIES) station, take the R4 line -direction Manresa- to Cerdanyola del Vallès station (25') then a short walk (1.2km or 0.8mi) crossing the town of Cerdanyola to NatuPark.

Lat: 4150194 • Long: 2.13109

wanna go there

The wildest rides

at PORT AVENTURA in Salou

pronounced "port ah-ven-two-rah"

#52

Forget the sugary Disney parks and alike, this is what you've been waiting for... a theme park like no other one. Rough and raw! The wildest rides (*Shambhala*, *Furius Baco*, *Dragon Khan* or the *Hurakan Condor*), the most amazing live shows and musicals with the cartoon characters

you know, breathtaking landscapes from México, the Far West, Polynesia and China. But this is not all, **Port Aventura** also has an aquatic park, called **Costa Caribe**, with fantastic rides too, so get ready to splash. It has plenty of restaurants and several hotels –should you want to stay longer. This theme park is so cool that even the train station that will get you there is named after it! •

Port Aventura

Av. Alcalde Pere Molas, km 2
43840 SALOU
Tel. +34 977 779 090

Schedule: 10am to 7pm (12pm in summer). Opens end of Mar to Oct and week-ends from Nov to early Jan. The aquatic park is open from end of May to Sep.

Getting there: From Sants (RODALIES) station, take the R16 line -direction Salou- to Port Aventura station (1h 45'), the park entrance is a short walk from the station.

www.portaventura.cat

Lat: 41.08607 • Long: 1.15077

My advice

It's really worthwhile -albeit a bit expensive- and kids will remember this day forever. For overnight stays at the park hotels: unless you book quite in advance, in summer it is very difficult to find a room. Alternatively, if you plan to get a two/three days ticket for Port Aventura, you can try a hotel nearby in Salou, but still it's going to be complicated during summer months or during Christmas. The key is booking quite in advance always. Get a combined ticket which includes: entry to the park for one day and return trip to the Port Aventura station, next to Salou. Buy it directly at the RODALIES station in Sants, west of the city. Ask for a "combined ticket Port Aventura" •

wanna go there

Secrets of a magic mountain

in MONTSERRAT

pronounced "moon-sah-rat"

Montserrat is an astonishing mountain range for it is so different from all others. From the distance, its silhouette is reminiscent of the toothed blade of a saw. And here you have the clue to its name, for the Catalan word Montserrat means *"sawn mountain"*. It is home of a Benedictine Monastery -with 1000 years of history. According to legend, the image of Our Lady of Montserrat –popularly know as the black madonna- was found in a cave nearby in the year 880! You can also listen, in the Basilica, to one of the most ancient boys' choir in Europe, the *Escolania de Montserrat*. Are you going to miss it? •

My advice

Transportation to Montserrat is one of the most spectacular features of this trip: either by rack railway or by cable car to overcome a steep gradient of 65 degrees to reach the monastery. Breathtaking! Once there, two funiculars will take you to the other emblematic sites on the mountain so you can enjoy some panoramical views of the nature park. The whole visit is an adventure: the transportation, the views, the monastery, the choir, even the museum as everything is surrounded in a mystical environment that will transport you into the past. Get a "TransMontserrat combined ticket" available at Plaça Espanya FCG station. Make sure you choose the right ticket, either to ride the rack railway or the cable car •

www.montserratvisita.com

Montserrat
Monestir de Montserrat
08199 MONTSERRAT
Tel. +34 938 777 701

Schedule: All year round. Check their website for detailed information on the different activities. The Choir does not perform in summer.

Getting there: From Plaça Espanya (FGC) station you have a train every 60', every day from 8:45am. Take the R5 line –direction to Manresa- and get off at Montserrat Aeri Station (for the cable car) or at Monistrol de Montserrat Station (for the rack railway). It takes 90' approx.
FREE for under-4s

Lat: 41.59316 • Long: 1.83737

wanna go there

Feel like a giant

at CATALUNYA EN MINIATURA in Torrelles

pronounced "cah-ta-loo-nee-ah an me-knee-ah-too-rah"

Catalunya en Miniatura is the only park where you can have a whistle-stop tour around Catalonia in a few short hours. A truly unique voyage! This is a family-run park, the largest in Europe, that displays miniature buildings and models along a 3km path that will take you through over 150 buildings and monuments located elsewhere in Catalonia. There's a miniature train that takes you on a 5' trip around the perimeter of the park for you to have an idea on what is where, then, you can stroll amid the typical ambiance of the most beautiful buildings in the country. An all-in-one in monument sightseeing! •

My advice

There's an adventure park with (tibetan bridges, zip lines and swinging logs) next to Catalunya en Miniatura called 'El Bosc Animat'. Reservation in advance is required. They operate in coordination with Catalunya en Miniatura but tickets have to purchased separately. Might be an interesting complementary activity if you plan to spend the whole day outside Barcelona •

catalunyaenminiatura.com

Catalunya en Miniatura
Can Balasch de Baix , s/n
08629 TORRELLES LLOBREGAT
Tel. +34 936 890 960

Schedule: 10am to 8pm Tue to Sun in Jul and Aug. to 6–7pm the rest of the year. Online tickets available.

Getting there: Take bus L62, operated by Soler i Sauret -green colour- (tel. +34 936 325 133) at the corner of Riera Blanca street with Travessera de les Corts which will take you straight to Torrelles de Llobregat, get off at the first stop in the town (ask the driver!) and the park is located 5' away. It takes 60' and it operates every hour most of the day.

FREE for under-3s

Lat: 41.35396 • Long: 1.97673

wanna go there

The world of wine making

at CAVES CODORNIU in Sant Sadurní d'Anoia

pronounced "cah-ves koh-dor-nee-oo"

Codorníu is the story of a wine-producing family that dates back to the 16th century that has become a worldwide wine producer producing a whopping 60 million bottles every year. In 1872, Codorníu produced his first bottle of cava. The vineyards of the region were devastated by the phylloxera plague, and the predominantly red vines were being replaced by large numbers of vines producing white grapes. After seeing the success of the *Champagne* region in France, Codorníu decided to create this dry sparkling wine, known as "*cava*", that has become the reason for the region's continued success •

My advice

Caves Codorníu
Avinguda Jaume Codorníu, s/n
08770 S. SADURNÍ D'ANOIA
Tel. +34 938 913 342

www.codorniu.com

Schedule: 9am to 5pm Mon to Fri, to 1pm on week-ends and public holidays. It is necessary to book in advance in order to check the winery's availability.

Getting there: From Plaça Catalunya (RODALIES) station take the R4 line -direction to Sant Vicenç de Calders- and get off at Sant Sadurní d'Anoia station (50'). Trains every 30'. From the station there is a 1.5km (0.9 mi) walk to the Codorníu estate. Taxis can be taken from the station.

FREE for under-7s

Lat: 41.43565 • Long: 1.79901

The visit is 90' and includes a guided tour through the beautiful Codorníu estate: from the magnificent Art-Nouveau winery buildings to the museum containing historic wine making relics. The visits are made in small groups and guided by an expert winemaker that will reveal all the secrets of these ancient techniques. The visit includes a trip through the underground cellars on a small train-like vehicle. With the temperature dropping several degrees, the underground caves -containing thousands of bottles of wine- and the semi-secluded rooms and halls spread here and there, make a wonderful attraction for kids. There is also a wine tasting session (for adults only, obviously!) •

wanna go there

See lions in the wild
at AQUALEON in Albinyana

pronounced "ah-coo-ah-leh-on"

Aqualeon is a safari park, an adventure park, a mini zoo and a water park all-in-one. Why not do a safari in a double-decker bus that will take you closer to lions, brown bears, zebras, antelopes and Siberian tigers? Then visit a mini zoo where you'll find meerkats, iguanas, chimpanzees, llamas, wallabies and many more. And finally, away from the wildlife, refresh yourself while sliding down a set of thrilling water toboggans. A complete day!... what more can you ask for? •

My advice

Visits outside the main season are also possible –and personally speaking– more desirable and less crowded. Animals are more active in cooler months hence it's easier to see them 'doing' something instead of just laying around. For those that have been on a real safari don't forget this is a tourist attraction, catch my drift? One of the most exciting rides is the horseback tours.... not alongside the lions, obviously! •

Aqualeon Safari
Finca les Basses s/n
43716 ALBINYANA
Tel. +34 977 687 656

www.aqualeon.es

Schedule: 10:30am to 6:30pm. Mon to Sun. Season mid Jun to mid Sep (rest of the year by appointment only). The Safari Bus departs every 30'. Tickets available online.

Getting there: From Sants (RODALIES) station take the R4 line -direction to Sant Vicenç de Calders- and get off at El Vendrell station (1h 10'). Trains every hour, at 25' past the hour. Aqualeon is 9km from the station. In summer, there is a regular bus service between the town and the park.

FREE for under-3s

Lat: 41.23102 • Long: 1.47813

wanna go there

A wild park in the wetlands

at PARC DELTAVENTUR in Deltebre

pronounced "park del-tah-ven-tour"

Deltaventur is located near the delta of the Ebre river, nearly 1000km long and one of the biggest rivers in Spain. The delta has several protected wetlands, beaches, marshes, salt pans, and estuaries that provide extensive habitats. Aside from strolling and bird watching, the park also offers a range of thrilling activities: kayaking, climbing walls, Tibetan bridges, canoeing, paintball, cycling, 4x4 tours, quads, archery, rock climbing, exploration of caves, punt boats and obstacle courses •

My advice

Parc Deltaventur
Road T-340 to Riumar, km 17
43580 DELTEBRE
Tel. +34 977 481 030 / 059 867

Schedule: 10am to 1pm and 3pm to 6pm Mon to Sun, to 7.30pm on weekends. Opens from Mar to Nov.

Getting there: This is the farthest attraction from Barcelona in this guide (~190km) and the tight timings in the links between train and bus schedules to go to Deltaventur might require an overnight stay. In order to simplify this and make it possible to be a 1-day activity I strongly recommend hiring a car in Barcelona instead. Approximate total journey time from Barcelona: 2h 45'.

Lat: 40.70831 • Long: 0.81431

www.parcdeltaventur.com

Minimum admittance age is 6 y.o. English/French speaking instructors are available at Deltaventur Park. Aside from visiting the park, should you drive there, don't forget to visit the wetlands area nearby as well as the Natural Park. This is a rice producing area, buy some "arroç bomba" (pronounced '*ah-ros bomb-ah*') a local variety of rice which makes for delicious "paellas". If you are planning to stay overnight in the area, don't forget to visit Tarragona, the old Roman capital. It has an amphitheatre, a large aqueduct and the old city walls... The remains are some of the best preserved Roman remains in this area of Europe. In summer there are historical re-enactments offering an exciting insight to Tarragona's Roman past. Have a look at www.tarragonaturisme.cat •

wanna go there

Watch eagles fly

at CIM D'ÀLIGUES in Sant Feliu de Codines

pronounced "seem dah-lee-guess"

Cim d'Àligues (Eagle's Peak) is a centre created for the study, breeding, exhibition and free-flight of birds of prey. From the big –such as eagles, vultures, buzzards, hawks, kites or goshawks- to the small –like owls and owlets- all these birds of prey can be found at Cim d'Àligues. Two main activities can be enjoyed there: a visit to the birds in the enclosures' area and a free-flight exhibition –the main attraction. The visit to the enclosures' area includes a brief explanation on general concepts about these birds: their diet, behaviour, habitats where they live, etc. The free flight-exhibition is performed twice a day, check for schedules on their website •

My advice

Unfortunately the guided visit is only offered in Catalan but the some of the keepers can answer questions in English too. Apart from being a very educational visit, it's very impressive to see these big birds, especially the hawks, performing low flights in front of the visitors to catch the baits thrown by their trainers. The exhibition is an hour long. Note that, for obvious reasons, the Cim d'Àligues activities are very weather dependant, so it's best to call them before making the trip •

www.cimdaligues.com

Cim d'Àligues
Paratge del Pi Solitari s/n
08182 S. FELIU DE CODINES
Tel. +34 938 662 648

Schedule: Very advisable to check their website or call ahead. During the summer they open from noon to 8pm Tue to Sun. The rest of the year the schedule varies. Closed from 1st to 15th Jul and 15th Dec to 15th Jan.

Getting there: Sagalés Bus (tel. 902 130 014 –local nbr) operates a regular line departing daily from Passeig de Sant Joan 52 in Barcelona. Buses from 7am. It takes about 75' to reach the town of Sant Feliu de Codines, from there, there's short walk (800 metres or ½ mi) to Cim d'Àligues

FREE for under-3s

Lat: 41.69522 • Long: 2.17356

wanna go there

Help to save a turtle
at the C.R.A.R.C. in Masquefa

CRARC stands for "Recovery Centre of Amphibians and Reptiles of Catalonia"

Over 230 million years among us! The C.R.A.R.C. is an institution dedicated to the rehabilitation of wildlife in order to return it to its natural habitat, and to promote scientific research and environmental education. It deals with amphibians and reptiles such as turtles, salamanders, frogs, crocodiles, lizards and iguanas. The keepers -Quim, Albert, Paqui and Isabel- are always thrilled to explain interesting stuff about these animals to the visitors of the centre •

My advice

The Centre is designed much like a mini-zoo: a path along which visitors can walk on their own and at their own pace while watching the animals. They do not offer guided tours but keepers are around and available for questions. To make sure there will be English speaking keepers is best to call in advance, but remember this is a scientific institution not a tourist attraction •

www.crarc-comam.net

C.R.A.R.C.
Santa Clara, s/n
08783 MASQUEFA
Tel. +34 937 726 396

Schedule: Week-ends only. From 10am to 1pm. Sat also from 4pm to 8pm. All year round.

Getting there: From Plaça Espanya (FGC) station take line R6 -direction to Igualada- and get off at Masquefa. It takes around 60' (22 stops) and there are trains every hour from Mon to Sun. Once at Masquefa, the CRARC is 5' away from the station. Return trips are twice each hour.

FREE for under-5s

Lat: 41.49909 • Long: 1.81465

wanna go there

Monkeysitting!

at FUNDACIÓ MONA in Riudellots de la Selva

pronounced "foon-dah-see-oh moh-nah". 'mona' being Catalan for female monkey

Some time ago, the Animal Planet Channel brought us the *"Monkey World Rescue Centre"* TV series, remember? Well, we in Catalonia have our very own apes' rescue centre called **Fundació Mona**. At this centre –albeit smaller and much less known than *Monkey World*– you have the possibility of visiting our primate cousins and to enjoy a small group guided visit while learning fascinating facts about them. You'll see mostly chimpanzees and macaques but also the odd gorilla and monkey here and there. Don't forget to get your MONA t-shirt or MONA mascot before you go •

My advice

This is not an animal exhibition centre but a rescue and research facility so visits are only by appointment. Visits are conducted in very small groups and they last around 2 hours during which an experienced keeper will accompany you through the facility which comprises a 5600m² chimpanzee outdoor area, an enclosures' area and various macaques areas. Visits can be also conducted in English or French. Do request it when making your appointment. Note that Riudellots is very (very!) close to Girona, you might want to combine this activity with a visit to this magnificent medieval city. Girona is considered -disputedly!- the second 'capital' of Catalonia and I personally love it. You shouldn't miss it •

www.fundacionmona.org

Fundació MONA
Carretera de Cassà, s/n
17457 RIUDELLOTS LA SELVA
Tel. +34 972 477 618

Schedule: Visits by appointment only. Generally, schedules for visits in English or French are mornings and afternoons during week days. In Jul and Aug also on week-ends.

Getting there: From Passeig de Gràcia (RODALIES) station, take a Regional Express train -direction to Portbou/Cerbere- and get off at Riudellots station (1h 30'). There are trains every two hours starting at 7am. Once in Riudellots, Fundació Mona is 15' away from the station.

FREE. but help the centre by making a small donation!

Lat: 41.89428 • Long: 2.85696

wanna go there

Become master of the castle

at the CASTELL DE CARDONA in Cardona

pronounced "cas-tel dah car-doh-nah"

Cardona is an important medieval town in Catalonia. Its castle, the *Castell de Cardona*, dates from the year 886 and is one of the best preserved. The dukes of Cardona, owners of the castle –and most of the lands around too!- became the most important family of the *Crown of Aragon*. This town is also famous for the salt mines. Salt was a precious commodity in the Middle Ages and Cardona was a major producer of this mineral. Nowadays the old mines have been transformed into a major attraction. The *Salt Mountain Cultural Park*, as it's called, offers a guided tour at a depth of 86m inside the galleries of the Salt Mountain, where the various spectacular folds and seams of the deposit and diversity of minerals are displayed in all their splendour •

My advice

Do not forget to visit the Church of Sant Miquel and the town historic centre as well, with its little stone-paved streets, the nobles' palaces and residences, the church, the arches in the many small squares across the town... it'll make you feel inside a true medieval environment. Also, the Josep Arnau Salt Museum displays many art pieces made with salt as the base ingredient. Cardona has several fairs and other festivities during the year, if you can, try to visit during those days •

Cardona Històrica
17457 CARDONA
Tel. +34 938 692 475

Schedule: Due to the variety of activities, check website for detailed information.

Getting there: ALSA (tel. 902 422 242 -local nbr) operates a regular bus line to Andorra, passing through Cardona, which departs daily from Estació del Nord (stop located at Ali Bei, 80) at 6:30am and it takes about 1h 45' to Cardona (7 stops away). The last return bus is at 5:15pm.

FREE for under-12s (castle) and for under-2s (mines)

Lat: 41.91449 • Long: 1.68611

www.cardonaturisme.cat

wanna go there

A few more ideas

Granja Can Castellví

La Rierada - 08770 MOLINS DE REI
www.cancastellvi.com (*in Catalan*) - Tel. +34 936 800 239 / +34 670 351 650
Hours: 11am to 2pm on week-ends and public holidays. Closed in August.

Granja Can Castellví is a family-run farming business near Barcelona that, on week-ends, offer urban families the chance to mingle with the animals helping the farmers feed and clean them. They have pigs, goats, different types of cocks and chickens, ponies, rabbits and even Australian emus –a relative of the ostriches. You can visit the farm, feed the animals and ride the ponnies. You'll be able to cuddle a cute bunny too! They have a restaurant service ●

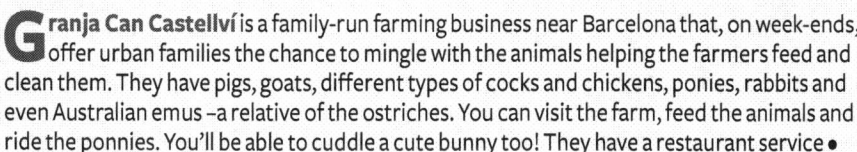

Indoor Karting Barcelona

Laureà Miró, 434 (N-340) - 08980 SANT FELIU DE LLOBREGAT
www.indoorkartingbarcelona.com - Tel. +34 936 857 500
Hours: 4pm to 9pm Mon to Fri, 10am to 9pm Sat and Sun and public holidays.

How much fun is indoor karting! A 500m (550 yards) asphalt track, pit stops, fast and slow curves, a downhill straight, elevation changes and a real-like finishing line are waiting for you, a great way to have fun and let tomorrow's budding stars shine. Receive your assignments, get your helmet, balaclava and race suit, and head to the briefing room for a short safety briefing. Then, compete against your self and against others. Learn the line of the racecourse, accelerate around the chicane turns and find your chance to pass on the hairpin turns ●

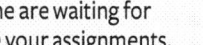

Canal Olímpic de Catalunya - EquaCat

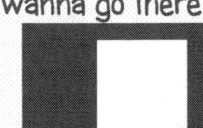
Avinguda Canal Olímpic s/n - 08860 CASTELLDEFELS
www.canalolimpic.com - Tel. +34 936 362 896
Hours: 10am until sunset, Mon to Sun all year round.

EquaCat, also known as "*Canal Olímpic de Catalunya*", is an installation built on the occasion of the 1992 Olympic Games as a headquarters for holding the Olympic canoeing competitions. The canal is 1.2km long, 130m wide and 4m deep and holds 450,000m² of fresh water. It's surrounded by a 2.7km road where land-based activities can take place. Nowadays, it's used for recreational activities such as canoeing, kayaking, windsurfing, row boats and *Optimist* (sailing dinghy) in the canal, and bicycling, skating and jogging in the road around ●

HOSPITAL DE LA
SANTA CREU I
SANT PAU
ARQUITECTE
LLUÍS DOMÈNECH I MONTANER

PATRIMONI
DE LA HUMANITAT
UNESCO 1997

ZOO

Key spots...

Use this section to easily find the key landmarks and monuments in the **central area of Barcelona**. A very brief description is added so you know what it's about. Locate them in the map in the next page.

01- Arc de Triomf: an impressive arch built in reddish brickwork in the Moorish Revival style for the 1888 Universal Exhibition.

02- Casa Batlló: a remarkable modernist house designed by Gaudí with a façade decorated with broken ceramic tiles.

03- Casa Milà: known as 'La Pedrera', designed as well by Antoni Gaudí, is part of the UNESCO World Heritage Programme.

04 - Monument a Macià: a curious monument in the shape of a set of stairs upside down dedicated to Francesc Macià, former president of Catalonia.

05 - Catedral de la Santa Creu i Santa Eulàlia: also known simply as 'Catedral de Barcelona' an impressive Gothic cathedral dating from the 13th century, seat of the Archbishop.

06 - Museu de la Catedral: a key spot to learn about the city's history, religious art and the guilds that made this city.

07 - Museu Picasso: one of the most extensive collections of art work of artist Pablo Picasso. A must see!

08 - Palau de la Música Catalana: a very beautiful concert hall, declared a UNESCO World Heritage Site in 1997.

09- Museu del Calçat: showcasing an unusual collection of shoes and tools used in the trade.

10- Museu Frederic Marès: preserving the collections assembled by its founder, sculptor Frederic Marès.

11- Museu Diocesà: over 3,000 works of art, including sculptures, paintings, gold and silverware, ceramics, and a variety of religious clothing, from the Visigothic and Roman era until the 21st century.

12- Temple d'August: dating back to the 1st century AD is one of the most well-preserved aspects from city's Roman era.

13- Casa de l'Ardiacà: or Archdeacon's House, which contains interesting archaeological remains of the city's rich past.

14- MUHBA: the City's History Museum with remains and artefacts from the past 2,000 years.

15- Museu Barbier-Mueller d'Art Precolombí: devoted to the artistic legacy of the pre-Columbian cultures of the Americas

16- Museu de la Xocolata: many of the displays are chocolate sculptures, including various well-known city buildings.

Key **spots**...

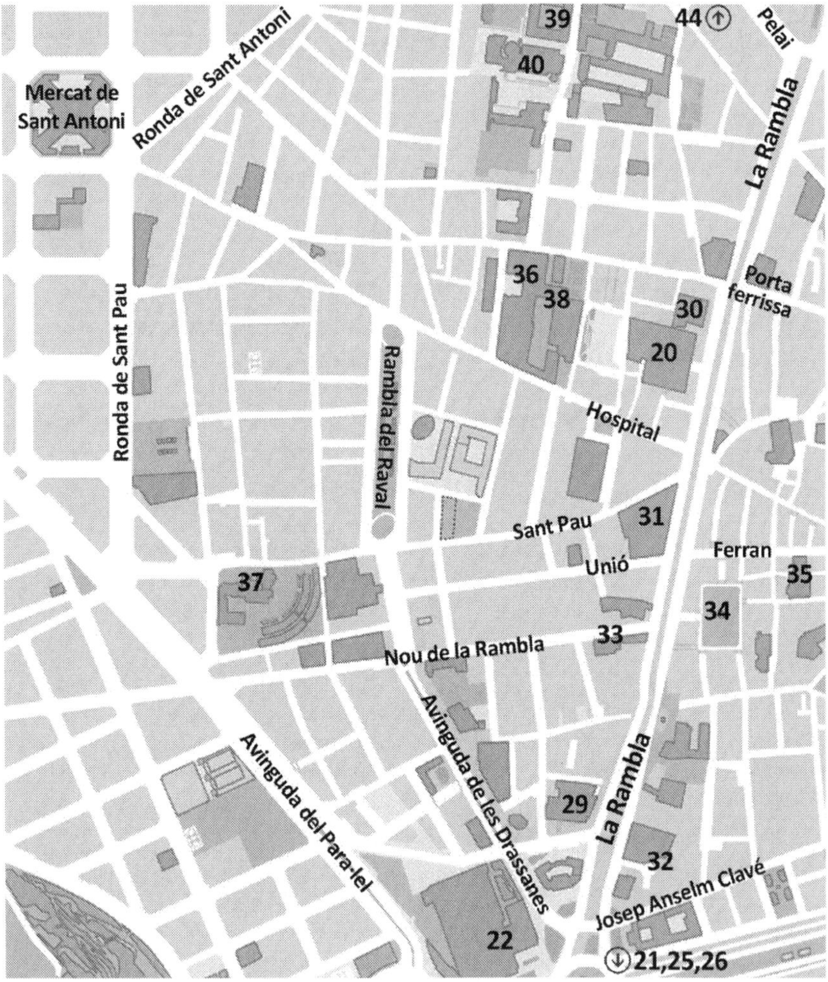

17- Barcelona Design Centre: promoting design for business excellence and a key factor for innovation.

18- Santa Maria del Mar: a medieval church built at the height of Catalonia's maritime and mercantile preeminence.

19- Mercat de Santa Caterina: a food market with an original multicoloured ceramics roof having the shape of wave

posed on an air structure of wood, which shelters all the stalls.

20- Mercat de St Josep "la Boqueria": the most famous food market in Barcelona. Originally a meat market founded in 1217.

21- Estàtua de Colom: the city's homage to Columbus, discoverer of the Americas, who returned to Barcelona to bring the good news.

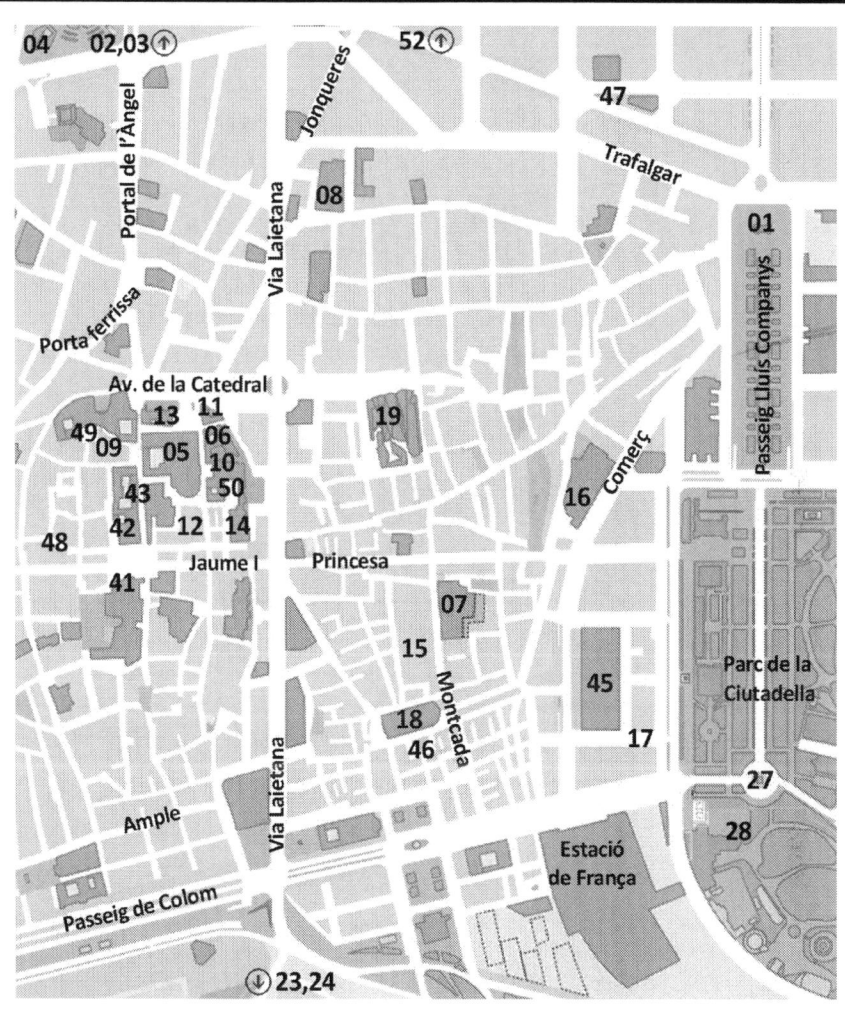

22- **Reials Drassanes – Museu Marítim**: shipyards, where the ships that made Catalonia a great sea power in the Mediterranean during the Middle Ages were built.

23- **Museu d'Història de Catalunya**: the history of Catalonia on display to make people aware of their shared heritage, and so help them identify with their national history.

24- **Torre de Jaume I**: this tower is the second-tallest aerial lift pylon in the world, and is a part of the Port Vell Aerial Tramway.

25- **Las Golondrinas**: Since 1888, these boats have chugged around the harbour, giving passengers a view of the city's rapidly changing seascape.

26- **Rambla de Mar – Maremagnum**: a promenade by the old harbour to one of the most visited mall centres in town.

27- **Parc de la Ciutadella**: Barcelona's most central park. The park includes a zoo, a lake, a large fountain and the Catalan Parliament.

28- **Zoo de Barcelona**: internationally known as the home of Snowflake, the only known albino gorilla that died on 2004.

29- **Centre d'Art Santa Mònica**: a public museum of contemporary art. It has no permanent collection but it hosts a number of travelling expositions of contemporary artists.

30- **Palau de la Virreina**: a Baroque palace that hosts museum exhibitions and cultural events.

31- **Teatre del Liceu**: an Opera house funded by private shareholders in 1847 considered to be one of best in the world.

32- **Museu de Cera**: no reputable city lacks its wax museum!

33- **Palau Güell**: one of the most luxurious mansions in the city commissioned by Count

Güell in 1880 and designed by Antoni Gaudí. Now is a private museum.

34- **Plaça Reial**: a very popular (and crowded) square in the city. Known by its famous clubs and outdoor areas. It's twinned with Plaza Garibaldi, in Mexico

35- **Església de la Mercè**: Beautiful Baroque church for the virgin of La Mercè which is the one venerated by the city.

36- **Antic Hospital de la Santa Creu**: one of Europe's earliest medical centres. There was a hospital on the site as early as 1024 and until the 1920s.

37- **Sant Pau del Camp**: a small medieval monastery located in what once was outside the city.

38- **Biblioteca de Catalunya**: the National Library, with over 3 million items located in the most amazing buildings.

39- **CCCB**: the most visited exhibition and arts centre in the city. It organizes and produces exhibitions, debates, festivals and concerts, lectures...

40- **MACBA**: the Barcelona Museum of Contemporary Art, a great building with a good permanent art collection.

41- Ajuntament de Barcelona: the City Hall, whose great hall, the Saló de Cent, has been a meeting point of the city's community since the 13th century.

42- Palau de la Generalitat: Catalonia's center of government, housing the President of the country.

43- Pont dels Sospirs: The most famous bridge in Barcelona in Carrer Bisbe, the "Pont dels Sospirs" or Bridge of Sighs frames the view and the gargoyles - originally used for drainage - loom overhead.

44- Universitat de Barcelona: a university closely tied to the history of Barcelona and Catalonia since 1402 when it's formally established by King Martí the Humane

45- Mercat del Born: a local landmark inspired by London's Covent Garden, it was the city's principal wholesale market until the mid-1970s.

46- Fossar de les Moreres: a memorial plaza with a torch of eternal flame where the defenders of the city were buried following the Siege of Barcelona in 1714.

47- Monument a Casanova: homage monument to Rafel de Casanova, mayor of Barcelona and commander in chief during the Siege of Barcelona in 1714.

48- El Call: Barcelona's Jewish Quarter, the main cultural hub in Catalonia from the 11th to the 14th centuries.

49- Plaça de Sant Felip Neri: one of the dark spots of the history of the city where many Barcelonians were executed at the end of the Spanish Civil war in 1939.

50- Palau Reial Major: a complex of historic buildings residence of the counts of Barcelona and, later, of the Kings of Aragon.

51- Arxiu de la Corona d'Aragó: since 1318 it's been the location of the Archive of the Crown of Aragon, a confederation made by the territories of Aragon, Catalonia and Valencia.

52- Casa Calvet: a building, designed by Antoni Gaudí, for a textile manufacturer which served as both a commercial property and a residence •

check
activity
#46

Cycling
in Barcelona

Barcelona is a very bike friendly city with more than a 180km of cycle lanes. The city's mild and sunny climate allow for all-year-long outdoor activities. Barcelona has its own public bicycle sharing system – very appropriately called **Bicing**– with over 6,000 bicycles and 150,000 users. But if you are a tourist or are only in town for a short while, this service is not right for you. It is designed for those people lucky enough to call Barcelona home.

Yet although Bicing is not accessible to you, there are other ways to rent a bicycle! Also, several companies offer group and private bike tours of the city and into the surrounding countryside and some high-end hotels even have comfort bikes for loaning gratis to guests.

Unlike American cities, where cyclists obey the same rules as vehicles, Barcelonian cyclists observe separate rules of the road. The general rule is to stick to marked bike paths, which variously and confusingly go with or against traffic, move from sidewalks to streets and back, are dedicated for bicycles only, or may be shared with taxis and buses.

Apart from giving you a visceral sense of the city, all that riding will burn up a lot of the *tapas* and *xocolata amb xurros* you are bound to eat during your holiday in the city •

Route**planner**

Just relax and let me take you through your visit to Barcelona.
I've prepared 7 different routes for you to enjoy.

1 **Monumental Barcelona**

2 **Relaxing day**

3 *Sun'n'beach* **day**

4 **Kid's day**

5 **A 'geeky' look 2 BCN**

6 **A 'fab' shopping day**

7 **A 'feeling sporty' day**

"see #00" refers to attractions and activities in this guide *(See index on page 220)*

Feel free to adapt the routes to your timing and your taste. I have scheduled each route to be made in 1 day but perhaps you want to take your time and split them in two, one day you do part of it, the next you finish the rest. In any case, I have included some timings in case you wonder *'where should I be at what time'* in order to finish the route within the same day.

Route**planner**

MONUMENTAL BARCELONA

By far the longest route proposed in this guide, but also the most spectacular. The starting point will be the Columbus monument in the old city and we'll end up in the evening in the bohemian neighbourhood of Gràcia.

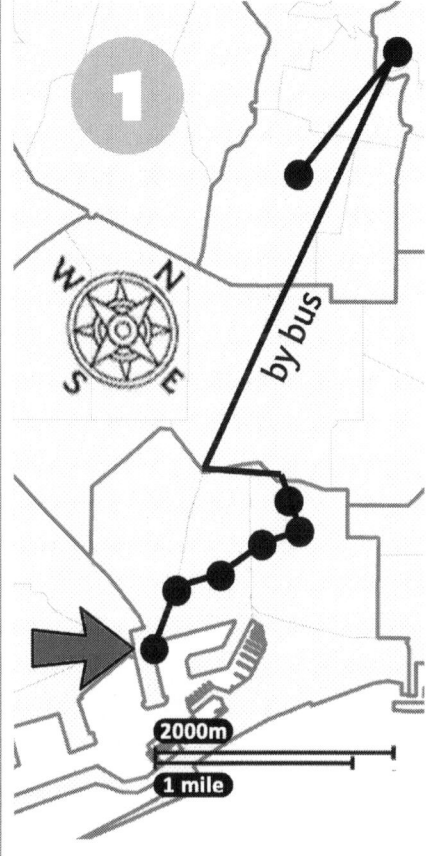

1. Columbus monument

This is the monument to the famous discoverer Christopher Columbus. Mistakenly, a lot of people think he's pointing to America, but he is in fact pointing towards the spot where Columbus ships were first sighted upon their return from the Americas. With the sea at your back, you'll be facing La Rambla, the most famous avenue in Barcelona. Since the city's origins 2250 years ago a lot of important historic events have happened there. To your immediate left, you'll see the **Drassanes** (#see 22), the royal shipyards, where ships were build until the late Middle Ages when the coastline was moved to where it is today.

2. La Rambla

La Rambla (see #11) is full of interesting characters, from painters to street performers, all kind of people selling stuff, people having a drink on the numerous terraces, locals going up and down about their business and many, many tourists. Ah! and a few pickpockets... watch out for them. Note the pavement resembles the waves of the sea. In the past, this avenue was full of florists, many coffee shop terraces and small press kiosks –as you can see, a few of those still exist- and it was (still is!) a preferred destination for Barcelonians to have a stroll on sunny Sunday mornings. It's something not to miss.

3. Plaça Reial

Plaça Reial is Catalan for "*Royal Plaza*". It's a square next to la Rambla and constitutes a well-known touristic meeting point, especially at night. On the square there are a large number of restaurants and some of the city's most famous clubs. It is also known for its many outdoor areas and is a popular meeting place during celebrations such as New Year's Eve, often being really crowded. It's twinned with Plaza Garibaldi, in Mexico DF, although the Plaça Reial is much smaller. Don't miss the elaborate patterns of the lanterns surrounding the square. They were designed by Antoni Gaudí. The shield you'll see in some of them is the coat of arms of the city of Barcelona. Exit the square to your left, and you'll reach Carrer Ferran.

4. Plaça Sant Jaume

Turn right on Carrer Ferran and walk 500m to the Plaça Sant Jaume where you'll find the Generalitat and the **Barcelona City Hall** (see #19): the epicentre of political power in Catalonia since its origins. The Generalitat is the equivalent to the White House in Washington or 10 Downing St in London, is where the President of Catalonia and his cabinet work. In front, the City Hall is where the Mayor's office is. Sometimes both institutions are governed by the same party... but sometimes they're not, and then is when it becomes interesting! Now take Carrer Llibreteria, a small street to the right of La Generalitat and then the third one to your left, Carrer Veguer... a few meters forward and you'll reach Plaça del Rei.

5. Plaça del Rei

The Plaça del Rei is the courtyard of the Palau Reial Major, the old palace of the Counts of Barcelona and the Kings of Aragon. It's worth visiting the Saló del Tinell (the royal palace's throne hall) and the Capella Reial de Santa Àgata. The Torre del Rei Martí (King Martin Watchtower) –five stories tall- was considered one of the tallest buildings in Europe when built in 1421; it sounds ridiculous nowadays, doesn't it? Some important ruins are exposed under this square, through the **Museu d'Història de la Ciutat** (see #10) you'll find an underground walk through excavations of Roman Barcelona. This is also the place where King Ferdinand and Queen Isabella welcomed Columbus when he returned from discovering America in 1492. And this is also the scenario of a less known later incident that year when a disgruntled peasant tried to kill King Ferdinand with a sword when he was coming down the staircase of Santa Àgata. The king was hurt in the neck and a popular believe is that one can still see three 'royal' blood drops on the third step of the staircase. Are they really there?

6. La Catedral

A stone's throw away (literally!) there is the Cathedral, or Saint Eulàlia's Cathedral to be precise, co-patron saint of the city. In 304 AD Eulàlia was a 13 year old Barcelonian that dared to defy the Roman prefect Dacius when he ordered the citizens to attend a rally where some poor souls were being sacrificed to stop Christianity spreading in the city. For this offence she was severely punished and then burnt at the stake. Then, as the legend goes, the flames attacked the soldiers that were around the pyre while the soul of Eulàlia came out of her mouth in the shape of a white pigeon that flew to Heaven. Pretty scary, eh? The cathedral was constructed during the 13th to 15th centuries and it's of Gothic style although the external façade was added during the 19th century. The roof is notable for its gargoyles, featuring a wide range of animals, both domestic and mythical. Inside the cathedral, you'll find a beautiful cloister, which encloses the Font de les Oques (Well of the Geese) with 13 white geese in remembrance of Eulàlia's age when she died.

Lunch in Barri Gòtic / Born

There are many places to lunch in the centre. Close to the cathedral my favourites are Mercè Vins (N'Amargós, 1) for an old fashion homely grandmother-style lunch in a tiny and friendly restaurant, Els Quatre Gats (Montsió, 3) for a truly Catalan cuisine experience, La Dolça Hermínia (Magdalenes, 27), seasonal Mediterranean cuisine with a touch of distinction to it at really competitive prices, Bun Bo Vietnam (Sagristans, 3) for a quick bite in an exotic Far East no-nonsense restaurant and, if you just fancy something to fill your tummy instead try Buenas Migas (Santa Clara, 2) for a focaccia or a piece of pizza and a shake or, at a 15 minute walk towards the harbour, Kapadokya (Fusteria, 6) for one of the best kebabs in town.

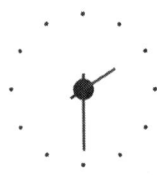

7. Parc de la Ciutadella

The **Parc de la Ciutadella** (see #02) came to be as part of a very sad story: when the Spanish King Philip V invaded Barcelona in 1714, he ordered to demolish the historical district of La Ribera to build a fortress –La Ciutadella- to keep firm control over its citizens. Fortunately nowadays it does no longer have that function. Now, it is characterized by being a very busy place,

crowded with tourists, and locals, who are usually going for a walk or taking their children to the special section for kids found near the upper margin of the park. The main attraction is the **Zoo de Barcelona** (see #01); with more than 7,000 animals. Near the zoo's entrance, the famous gigantic stone mammoth is to be seen.

8. Arc de Triomf

Leaving the Parc de la Ciutadella by the north exit, you'll be able to see an impressive archway structure: l'Arc de Triomf. This reddish brickwork arch in the Moorish Revival style was built for the 1888 Barcelona Universal Exhibition. But before walking to the arch, you might want to check Lolita Bakery (Portal Nou, 20), located in a small street to the left of the park is, for me, one of the best bakeries in the city where you can find delicious homemade brownies and cupcakes. Also notice that the **Chocolate Museum** (see #07) is very nearby. From the Arc de Triomf take a street to your left named Ronda Sant Pere towards Plaça Catalunya where we'll take a bus to Parc Güell. At about half way you'll find a statue to your right depicting Rafael de Casanova. He became mayor of Barcelona and commander in chief of Catalonia during the Siege of Barcelona until he was wounded in combat when commanding a counterattack of the Barcelona militia on the last day of siege, Sep. 11th, 1714, now the Catalan National Day, when thousands of citizens come to pay respect to this hero of the country's history. Once you reach Plaça Catalunya, in front of El Corte Inglés Shopping Center jump into the 28 bus that will take you to Park Güell. Ask the driver to let you know when to get off but for information it's roughly 40' - or some 14 stops.

9. Parc Güell

The **Parc Güell** (*see #34*) is a huge park in the north east part of the city where you can admire the genius of architect Antoni Gaudí. He designed it in 1900 and originally it had to be a housing development but in 1922 it ended up as a public park instead for all Barcelonians to enjoy. It's over 15 hectares and contains several worth seeing features: the dragon and stairs in the main entrance, the Nature square, the rose garden, the museum, the weird viaducts and the Turó de les Tres Creus, its highest point where you'll have a superb view of the city. Note you'll be entering the park by one of the side entrances and will make your way towards the main entrance, where the dragon and stairs are located.

10. Gràcia

After exiting Parc Güell by the main entrance, there's an easy-to-walk downhill slope towards the neighbourhood of Gràcia, at a few hundred meters. Gràcia was established in 1626 by Carmelites who built a convent there. It used to be a separate township until 1897 when it was annexed to Barcelona along with other villages. The neighbourhood is a bit off the beaten track, hence less crowded by tourists. The narrow streets create a very intimate ambience and there are plenty of small shops and many artisans. Students and artists make their home here, and everyone's welcome to hang out in its open air spaces, its cafes and bars. La Nena (*see section "The Best...for a sweet treat"*), a very popular place for sweets, chocolate, home made cakes and dairy products is here in Gràcia.

Dinner/snack in Gràcia

This neighbourhood has a magical atmosphere that invites to stay for dinner after a busy day. There are many (many!) small restaurants that offer a wide variety of food and cuisines. Among my favourite places are: La Llavor dels Origens (Ramon i Cajal, 12) to taste Catalan tapas at its best, Kibuka (Goya, 9 and Verdi, 64) magnificent Japanese cuisine and not expensive, Goliart (Progrés, 6) very good market kitchen in a cute restaurant, Ugarit (Bruniquer, 69) a superb Lebanese chain very popular among students, El Glop (Sant Lluís, 24) typical Catalan cuisine, and the best Mexican in town at Chido One (Torrijos, 30), not pretentious simply delicious. But again, there are too many to choose from ●

TORRIJOS STREET IN GRÀCIA

Route**planner**

2

RELAXING DAY

A relaxing day across the city, away from the uproar of the centre. The starting point will be Plaça Catalunya, the heart of the city, but we'll quickly move away to other districts of the city: Gràcia and Pedralbes

1. Plaça Catalunya

The Plaça Catalunya is considered to be the central point of Barcelona. This square is a main hub for public transportation in the city, it has a Tourist Information Office, a main police station under the square, several shopping centres around it (El Corte Inglés, el Triangle...), the Hard Rock Cafe in Barcelona, the famous avenues Passeig de Gràcia and La Rambla both start here, the busiest shopping street in Spain -Portal de l'Àngel- is next to the square. This route proposes starting with an escapade to one of the many parks in the city. I've chosen either the Parc Güell or the Parc del Laberint (The Maze's park). For the first one, take bus 28 in front of El Corte Inglés shopping centre and it will take you to one of the side entrances of the park. For the second one, take metro L3 (green) to Mundet (30') and walk 10' to the park.

2a. Parc Güell

The **Parc Güell** (see #34) is a huge park in the north east part of the city where you can admire the genius of architect Antoni Gaudí. He designed it in 1900 and originally it had to be a housing development but in 1922 it ended up as a public park instead for all Barcelonians to enjoy. It's over 15 hectares and contains several worth seeing features:

the dragon and stairs in the main entrance, the Nature square, the rose garden, the museum, the weird viaducts and the Turó de les Tres Creus, its highest point where you'll have a superb view of the city.

2b. Parc del Laberint

The **Parc del Laberint** (see #36) is the oldest and most beautiful park in Barcelona. It was created at the end of the 1700s -just after the French Revolution- and it belonged to the Desvalls family, a very rich aristocratic family that donated it to the city in 1967. The park consists of several areas which includes, of course, the Laberint (the maze) located at the centre of the park, a 750 meter (820-yard) long maze created from pollarded cypress trees that gives its name to the park. In the centre is a statue of Eros, the god of love.

3. Gràcia

Now let's go for a stroll in the neighbourhood of Gràcia. After exiting Parc Güell by the main entrance, there's an easy-to-walk downhill slope towards the neighbourhood of Gràcia, at a few hundred meters. If you decided to visit the Parc del Laberint instead, take again the metro at Mundet stop and get off at Fontana (15'). Gràcia was established

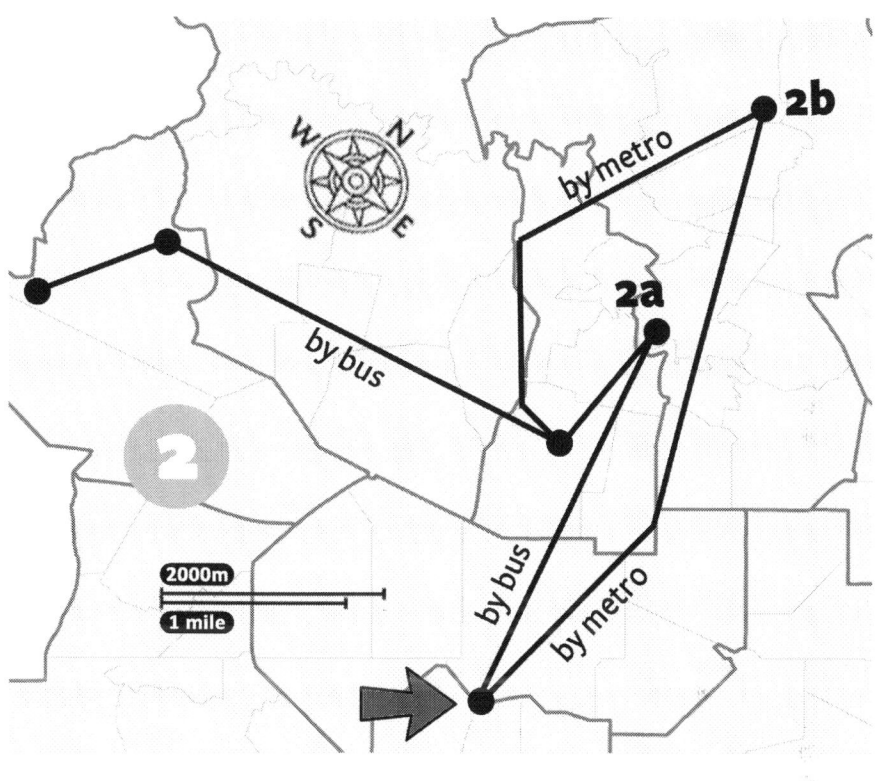

in 1626 by Carmelites who built a convent there. It used to be a separate township until 1897 when it was annexed to Barcelona along with other villages. The neighbourhood is a bit off the beaten track, hence less crowded by tourists. The narrow streets create a very intimate ambience and there are plenty of small shops and many artisans. Students and artists make their home here, and everyone's welcome to hang out in its open air spaces, its cafes and bars. La Nena (see the section **"The Best...for a sweet treat"**), a very popular place for sweets, chocolate, home made cakes and dairy products is here in Gràcia.

Lunch in Gràcia

This neighbourhood has a magical atmosphere that invites to stay for lunch or for dinner. There are many small restaurants that offer a wide variety of food and cuisines. Among my favourite places are: La Llavor dels Origens (Ramon i Cajal, 12) to taste Catalan *tapes* at its best, Kibuka (Goya, 9) Japanese cuisine and not expensive!, Goliart (Progrés, 6) good market kitchen, Ugarit (Bruniquer, 69) a superb Lebanese chain very popular among students, El Glop (Sant Lluís, 24) typical Catalan cuisine, and the best Mexican in town at Chido One (Torrijos, 30), not pretentious simply delicious.

Route**planner**

4. Monastir de Pedralbes

Get to Gran de Gràcia street, the major avenue in the district, and take bus 22 to the Creu de Pedralbes (35') –ask the driver where to get off. From there is a 5' walk to the Monastir de Pedralbes, a Gothic monastery founded in 1326 by King James II. The monastery is an impressive set of buildings that can be visited to see how nuns lived in the Middle Ages. It also has one of the best museums of Romanesque art. The best part is the cloister, one of the more peaceful and beautiful spots one can find in Barcelona.

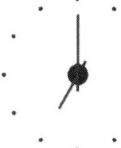

5. Parc Cervantes

From the monastery, taking again bus 22 to the end of the line (merely 15'), you'll reach **Parc Cervantes** (*see #43*). This park is worth visiting especially from May to July since one can appreciate the huge collection of rosebushes of some 200 species that, when blooming, produce a unique atmosphere full of colour and a zillion aromas. Next to the park there are several bus lines and a metro to go back to the centre. Note that in winter, as it gets dark much earlier, so the park will close quite early (around 6*ish*) ●

SUN'N'BEACH DAY

Visiting the magnificent beaches of one of the newest districts in the city: the Olympic Port area

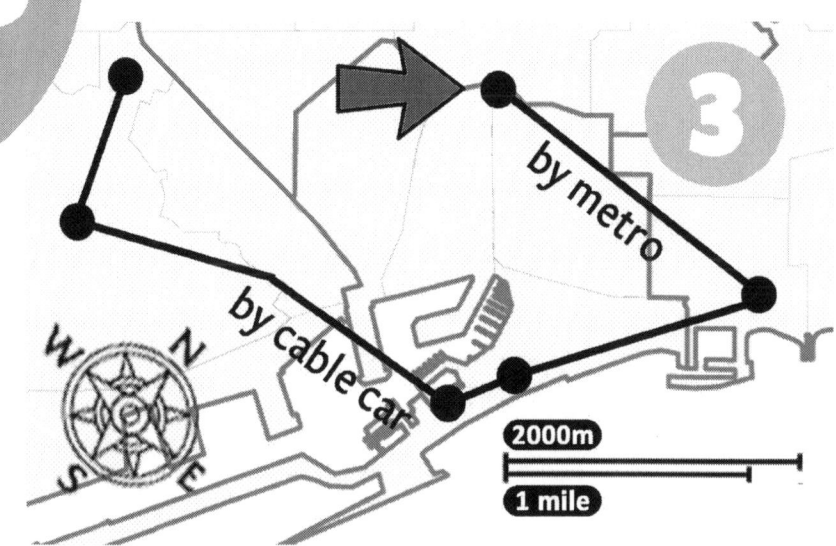

1. Plaça Urquinaona

The Plaça Urquinaona is 5' away from Plaça Catalunya. From there take metro L4 (yellow) to Ciutadella/Vil·la Olímpica (10'). The Nova Icària beach is 15' away from this stop, to the left of the twin towers: the Mapfre tower and the Hotel Arts tower.

2. Platja de la Nova Icària

The Platja de Nova Icària is one of the many beaches in Barcelona. I've chosen this one because is located in a very nice spot of the coast, next to the Olympic Port, an area packed with restaurants to have a lunch after the beach. The beaches are spacious and made of fine golden sand –yet not quite like the Caribbean! The shore is quite shallow and the seabed is sandy, hence the reason why the water is not very transparent, especially in days when the sea current is strong. Always obey the instructions of the beaches. "Green" means you can safely take a swim, "yellow" that you must be very careful -either because of strong sea currents, floating jellyfish...- and "red" that is dangerous to enter the sea so the water is a no-go area that day, got it? OBEY these instructions for your own safety.

Lunch in the Olympic Port

This neighbourhood was radically transformed in 1992, after the Olympic Games. Today, the restaurant offer is quite amazing. Note that this is a trendy area so many restaurants may be a bit pricey, especially the fancy ones. There are though three places I'd like to highlight: Crêperie Bretonne Annaick (2' from the Hotel Arts tower), with exceptional crêpes either sweet or savoury, you'll find a filling to satisfy your craving and it's very inexpensive, Ca la Nuri

(Passeig Marítim de la Barceloneta, 55) a bit pricey but with the best paelles you can find, and El Rebujito de Moncho's (next to the Hotel Arts tower), part of a very famous chain of restaurants in the city, an informal and colourful place where you can enjoy a truly Mediterranean meal with plenty of fish and seafood or, if you prefer, try some of their delicious tapes instead.

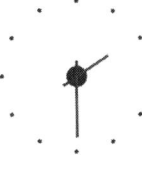

3. Stroll to La Barceloneta

After lunch, a stroll to La Barceloneta neighbourhood is a pleasure. Take a walk by the seafront promenade towards the W Hotel, which everybody calls the 'sail hotel' since it has a shape that reminds one of a sail of a ship. The more traditional part of the Barceloneta neighbourhood is located near the end. This neighbourhood was created in 1753 when the first stone on land won from the sea was laid. The first settlers of this new neighbourhood were mainly fishermen, due to its proximity to the sea began to build their homes here.

4. Ride on the cable car

Ready for some action now? Why not take a ride in a cable car to admire the city from above? Walk to the **cable car tower** (see #17) next to the Sant Sebastià beach and ride the cable car -the Telefèric de Montjuïc- to the top of the hill. A trip not for the faint hearted: 70m above the sea level!

5. Jardí Botànic

Being now in Montjuïc, a visit to the **Jardí Botànic** (see #30) -the botanical garden- it's very appropriate. To get there, after leaving the cable car, walk

Route**planner**

about 200 metres to the Avinguda Miramar and at the Av.Miramar/Pl.Carlos Ibañez bus stop take bus 150 and get off after four stops (at Estadi Olímpic stop). Then there's a short 10' uphill walk to the Jardí Botànic. The Barcelona botanical garden specializes in plants and communities from those areas of the world with Mediterranean climates, from Chile to Australia, including of course those in the Mediterranean basin. These gardens provide a great sense of openness and space that it's truly calming and inspiring. Being outdoors though, this is not really a winter activity so if it's close to sunset you might want to skip this step and go to the next one.

Snack in Las Arenas

After the visit to the botanical gardens you can choose either to take a bus to descend the Montjuïc mountain towards Plaça Espanya (bus 13 will do!) or else to walk downhill -which is faster as the bus takes the long way to Plaça Espanya. If the weather is nice a walk is a pleasant journey and will allow you to admire some other sites that are located in this mountain such as the Olympic Stadium, the MNAC museum or the Poble Espanyol among many others. In any case, once you arrive to Plaça Espanya, head to the Las Arenas Shopping Center. You can't miss it because it's located in a former bullring, hence the building it's... round! You'll find there, inside and around, up to 30 different restaurants to have a snack –or a light dinner.

6. La Font Màgica

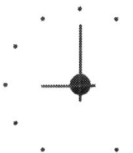

I bet you thought that was it for the day... but wait, there's still one more treat: **La Font Màgica** (*see #31*), a spectacular display of music, water acrobatics and lights. After sunset, the fountains located in the avenue Reina Maria Cristina –west of Plaça Espanya and a few minutes walk from Las Arenas– offer a (free!) open air show for everybody to enjoy. Check the "Activities and attractions" section for details as performances are not daily •

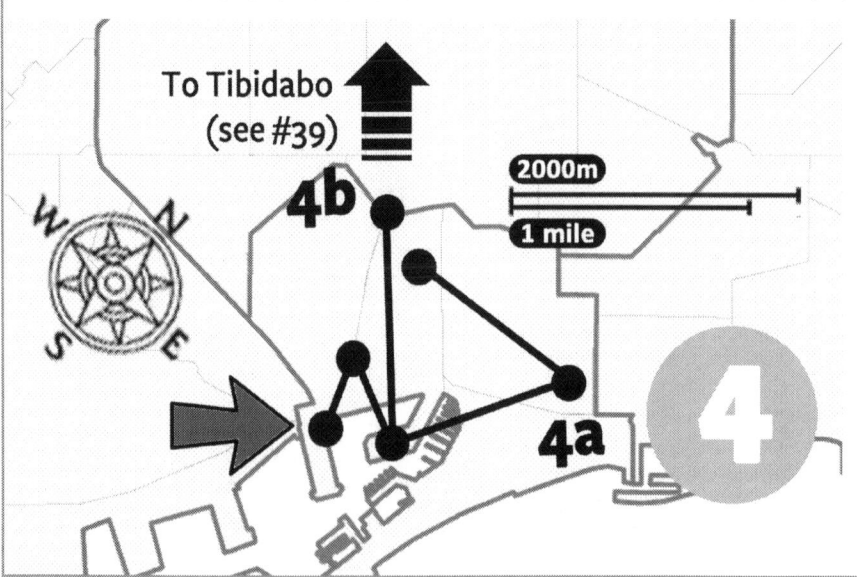

To Tibidabo
(see #39)

2000m
1 mile

4b

4a

4

KID'S DAY

Fun activities all day long:
wax museum, aquarium
and the zoo -or the fun fair.

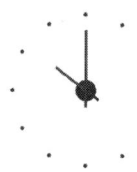

1. Columbus Monument

This is the monument to the famous discoverer Christopher Columbus. Mistakenly, a lot of people think he's pointing to America, but he is in fact pointing towards the spot where Columbus ships were first sighted upon their return from the Americas. With the sea at your back, you'll be facing La Rambla, the most famous avenue in Barcelona. Since the city's origins 2,250 years ago a lot of important historic events have happened there. To your immediate left, you'll see the **Drassanes** (*see #22*), the royal shipyards, where ships were build until the late Middle Ages when the coastline was moved to where it is today.

2. Museu de Cera

At La Rambla, you'll spot the entrance to the back-street leading to the wax museum when you locate an old kiosk with a wax figure next to it. The **Museu de Cera** (*see #08*) has over 360 human-like wax figures representing historical and entertainment personalities: musicians, painters, clowns, artists, emperors, kings and queens, thieves, warriors, murderers, popes... and of course, the chamber of horrors! Before leaving don't forget to have refreshment in the Bosc de les Fades (*the Forest of the Fairies*)... it's a charming place!

3. Aquarium de Barcelona

Back in La Rambla, face the sea and walk towards the Columbus monument again. There's a modern wooden bridge to your left, where La Rambla meet the sea... cross it. Now you're in the Maremagnum Shopping Centre and the Aquarium is located here, next to the IMAX theatre. The **Aquarium de Barcelona** (*see #03*) is one of Europe's biggest marine leisure and education centres and the most important concerning Mediterranean species. You'll find here spectacular sharks, giltheads, rays and many more.

Lunch

You're now in the old harbour neighbourhood and this is a very touristy area. Albeit there are plenty of restaurants around, they can be pricey and service might not be what one's expecting. If you're in for a snack instead you'll find also many fast-food like places. However, and given we're next bound for either the Barcelona

Route**planner**

Zoo or perhaps Tibidabo, I'd suggest to lunch elsewhere. If you've decided to go for the zoo, try Tasca i Vins (Av. Marquès de l'Argentera, 13) a rustic place serving typical Catalan dishes or perhaps Ugarit (Comerç, 29) a Syrian restaurant serving delicious meat and vegetable dishes. Both are next to the Estació de França, a main train station. If you're heading for Tibidabo instead, the choice is wider as you have to cross town anyway. Have lunch somewhere on your way towards Plaça Catalunya. Where?, check my recommendation in the route "Monumental Barcelona".

4a. Tibidabo fun fair

The **Tibidabo** (see #39), is the oldest fun fair in Catalonia. It was inaugurated in 1901 and it's located in the top of the mountain overlooking the city, to the north (of the map). This is an 'old-style' amusement park: compact and with attractions geared towards the younger ones. Don't expect to find the latest-rides-in-the-market, although it has over 25 thrilling rides such as roller coasters, a swinging lookout tower, or the Hall of Mirrors. To get there fast, get to Plaça Catalunya and take Tibibus T2A. The bus runs from 10.15 am onwards every day that the amusement park is open. Tibibus fare is reimbursed when you hand in your bus ticket at the park's ticket office.

4b. Zoo de Barcelona

The **Zoo de Barcelona** (see #01) is ranked among the top zoos in Europe and has open enclosures, allowing you to almost touch the animals. There is an infant zoo where children can be introduced to various animals. It houses over 7,000 animals in a 74 acre park. The main attractions are the dolphinarium, a brand new penguin enclosure featuring the endangered Humboldt species and an underground tunnel for observation. If you've decided to lunch in the area I've recommended above, the Zoo is a mere 5' walk, inside the Parc de la Ciutadella.

Snack

If you've chosen to visit the zoo, I recommend yet a last activity for this day: to have a very typical local kids' treat. For generations parents have taken their kids to one of the granges –cafes that serve traditional desserts such as delicious chocolate and xurros, which are sweet fried pastries similar to doughnuts– across the city. Unfortunately, nowadays many granges are long gone but there are still a few remaining ones such those at Petritxol street, in the old town, where places like La Pallaresa or La Dulcinea have been serving xurros for over half a century. This tiny pedestrian-only street is located off the Plaça del Pí, next to La Rambla. Another great place for sweet treats in the old town is Caelum (see the section "**The Best…for a sweet treat**") ●

short for "Barcelona"

A 'GEEKY' LOOK 2 BCN!

Learning stuff while playing around in some very special museums.

5

1. Plaça Catalunya

The Plaça Catalunya is considered to be the central point of Barcelona. This square is a main hub for public transportation in the city, it has a Tourist Information Office, a main police station under the square, several shopping centres around it (El Corte Inglés, el Triangle...), the Hard Rock Cafe in Barcelona, the famous avenues Passeig de Gràcia and La Rambla both start here, the busiest shopping street in Spain -Portal de l'Àngel- is next to the square. I've chosen either the Egyptian Museum or the MUHBA, the City History Museum. Both are fairly close so I'd recommend walking there.

2a. Museu Egipci

To get there take Passeig de Gràcia and turn right into València street. The **Museu Egipci** (*see #21*) has one of the finest collections of Ancient Egyptian artefacts in Europe spanning 3,000 years of Nile-drenched culture. Outstanding pieces include some fragments from the Sixth Dynasty Tomb of Iny, a bronze statuette of the goddess Isis, and mummified cats, baby crocodiles and

falcons. If after visiting this museum it's still too early to lunch, try visiting **La Pedrera** (*see #20*) –which is at a stone's throw.

Lunch after Museu Egipci

If in l'Eixample you might want to try Merendero Campechano (see the section *"The Best...to have a quick bite"*) a genuine barbeque-style restaurant, Tapas 24 (Diputació, 269) for delicious Catalan tapes, or for a deluxe treat try Thai Gardens (Diputació, 271), a unique Thai experience in the cosiest and prettiest restaurant in Barcelona. Not for a shoe string budget though!

2b. MUHBA

To get there head towards the heart of old city (Barri Gòtic), south-east from Plaça Catalunya. The old city is tricky to walk due to the maze of small pedestrian streets so better let your parents check a 'proper' map to get there. In any case, it's next to Plaça Sant Jaume, the main square where the Generalitat and the City Hall are located. The **MUHBA**, the Barcelona City History Museum (*see #10*), takes you on a journey through Barcelona's 2,000 year history. From the first Roman settlement to the Middle Ages remains to the modern and vibrant city that Barcelona is today. The MUHBA has several sites spread across the city, the one I suggest to visit is the one containing the remains of the Roman city as well as a series of splendid monuments which provide an insight into medieval Barcelona. If after visiting this museum it's still too early to lunch, try visiting the **Museu del Mamut** (see #18) -yes, mammoth!- close to MUHBA.

Lunch after MUHBA

There are many places to lunch in the Barri Gòtic. Some of my favourites are Mercè Vins (N'Amargós, 1) for an old fashion homely grandmother-style lunch in a tiny and friendly restaurant, Els Quatre Gats (Montsió, 3) for a truly Catalan cuisine experience, or La Dolça Hermínia (Magdalenes, 27), seasonal Mediterranean cuisine with a touch of distinction to it at really competitive prices.

3. Museu de la Ciència

From Barcelona's nearly 70 museums, the **Museu de la Ciència** or CosmoCaixa (see #38) is arguably the coolest and more entertaining one. In this museum, everybody, young or old can enjoy themselves and learn a lot about Natural Sciences, trying out many things, and even experience tropical rain. The museum showcases items and devices demonstrating various examples of physical phenomena in an amusing manner. At CosmoCaixa you won't see a single 'do not touch' sign anywhere like it usually happens in a museum – CosmoCaixa is a very interactive place where you're encouraged to touch and experiment instead. And its very inexpensive (good thing!)

Snack

After so much food for the brain now it's time for some food for the tummy! A visit

to the neighbourhood of Gràcia will land you in an area full of small cafes and *granges* –cafes that serve traditional desserts. To get to Gràcia from CosmoCaixa, walk downhill to Passeig de la Bonanova and take bus 22 direction Plaça Catalunya and stop in Plaça Gal·la Placídia –about 10 stops, depending where you got on the bus. The neighbourhood is a bit off the beaten track, hence less crowded by tourists. The narrow streets create a very intimate ambience and there are plenty of small shops and many artisans. La Nena (see the sections "***The Best… for a sweet treat***"), a very popular place for sweets, chocolate, home made cakes and dairy products is here in Gràcia •

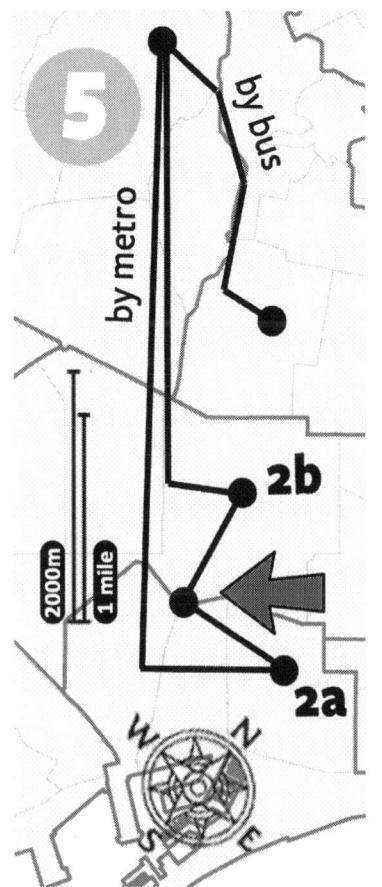

A *'FAB'* SHOPPING DAY

This route is for you shopping lovers...
"shop 'til you drop", that's the motto.

1. Plaça de la Catedral

The Plaça de la Catedral is located in the old city, the Barri Gòtic, and it's a perfect place to start this shopping escapade. But when we say shopping, what we really mean is clothes, shoes, handbags and accessories, isn't it?. Well, park everything else because today is that day. Let's shop until we drop in one of the fashion warehouses of Europe that is Barcelona. Indeed the city has nearly one fifth of its turnover in this sector (40 billion €), with over 30,000 retail stores and 15 shopping centres spread across and around the city. With such vast number of stores and outlets it's not really possible, or practical, to define a route with specific points to shop in so I will focus on 'areas' instead. Good news: Barcelona ranks among the more affordable cities in Europe for this kind of shopping. Will you think so too?

2. Portaferrisa/Portal de l'Angel

From La Catedral, this area is only a 100m away (110 yards) and is full of stores, many from trendy brands from major groups such as Zara or Desigual as well as many smaller independent shops offering a wide range of items, from the young and rebellious to alternative styles. Don't simply stay in the main streets, venture into the smaller side streets too, you might be surprised. In this area you can also visit two El Corte Inglés department stores.

3. Pelai Street

Very close, Carrer Pelai has more of these well-known clothes and shoe brands shops while in the back-streets you'll find smaller and often more specialized shops. Also, you'll find El Triangle shopping centre in Plaça Catalunya, opposite to El Corte Inglés, with a huge Sephora store, the most innovating space for beauty in town, and a 100% lively space dedicated to beauty desires.

Check section "**Shopping**" (page 181) for a ton of information

Route**planner**

4. Passeig de Gràcia

This is 'the' main avenue for the luxurious brand boutiques we all know (but few can afford!): Armani, Louis Vuitton, Carolina Herrera, Cartier, etc. You will also find more reasonable priced stores of course but mostly from global brands (Guess, Diesel...). Rambla Catalunya, parallel to Passeig de Gràcia, has also a great variety of good stores –and less expensive! You're now in an area of the city called l'Eixample.

Lunch

I guess that today you won't want to waste much time with a fancy meal, right? There are plenty of cafes and restaurants in the area of l'Eixample where you can get a quick bite. Try Cornelia and Co. (see the section *"The Best...to have a quick bite"*) where you can have a light pasta dish, a salad... in a charming rustic environment, Ciutat Condal (Rambla Catalunya, 18) and Tapas 24 (Diputació, 269) both offer good *tapes* (or *tapas* in Spanish), or Citrus (Passeig de Gràcia, 44) Mediterranean cuisine with a warm atmosphere, elegant table dressings and good service yet inexpensive at lunch time.

5. Diagonal area

After lunch let's head to the Diagonal area where stores are open all day long. My advice would be to take a bus H6 on Diagonal to Pedralbes Shopping Centre (Diagonal, 609) probably the farthest I'd go for a shopping hunt, and walk your way back from there. In Pedralbes Centre, located in a black Rubik-cube like building, you'll find nearly 50 stores ranging from clothing to accessories. Next to it you'll find another El Corte Inglés. Once you've seen these, walk towards Plaça Francesc Macià. Half way you'll find L'Illa Diagonal Shopping Centre, the mecca for shopping in this area with more than 170 shops and a huge Decathlon store for those sports fans. Continue walking a bit more towards Plaça Francesc Macià. Once there, you'll find yet another El Corte Inglés and, on both sides of Diagonal avenue, plenty of up-market trendy clothes stores.

2000m

1 mile

Snack

I bet you've got swollen feet by now, fancy a rest while having a snack? If you're in Plaça Francesc Macià you can try Casa Danone for a delicious yoghourt –frozen or not– with different toppings and flavours. But if you're adventurous enough to still want to go on, get to the neighbourhood of Gràcia and visit La Nena a very popular place for sweets, chocolate, home made cakes and dairy products. Both places are featured in the section *"**The Best...for a sweet treat**"*.

6. Gràcia area

Finally, if you're not dead tired (and your credit card hasn't burnt yet) I'd head to Gràcia to hunt for those not-mainstream clothes and accessories that will make your wardrobe unique. You might want to take bus 27 in carrer Buenos Aires and stop in Av. Princep d'Astúries-Rambla del Prat (4 stops), then walk 2' to Gran de Gràcia street, the main artery in the neighbourhood. From there walk your way downwards towards Passeig de Gràcia not forgetting to scan the side streets too, especially those to your left, which will take you deep inside Gràcia. Needless to say there plenty of other areas and shopping centres in Barcelona. Today you've only seen a fraction of it! •

A 'FEELING SPORTY' DAY

If you like sports this is your day:
the Olympic complex,
the Camp Nou...

7

1. Plaça Catalunya

The Plaça Catalunya is considered to be the central point of Barcelona. This square is a main hub for public transportation in the city, it has a Tourist Information Office, a main police station under the square, several shopping centres around it (El Corte Inglés, el

Triangle...), the Hard Rock Cafe in Barcelona, the famous avenues Passeig de Gràcia and La Rambla both start here, the busiest shopping street in Spain -Portal de l'Àngel- is next to the square. From here you can go to Camp Nou by a combination of train+metro or directly by bus, albeit it'll take a bit longer yet travelling above ground will allow you to see more of the city. By bus, walk 5' to Plaça Universitat and take bus 54 in front of the university building direction to Campus

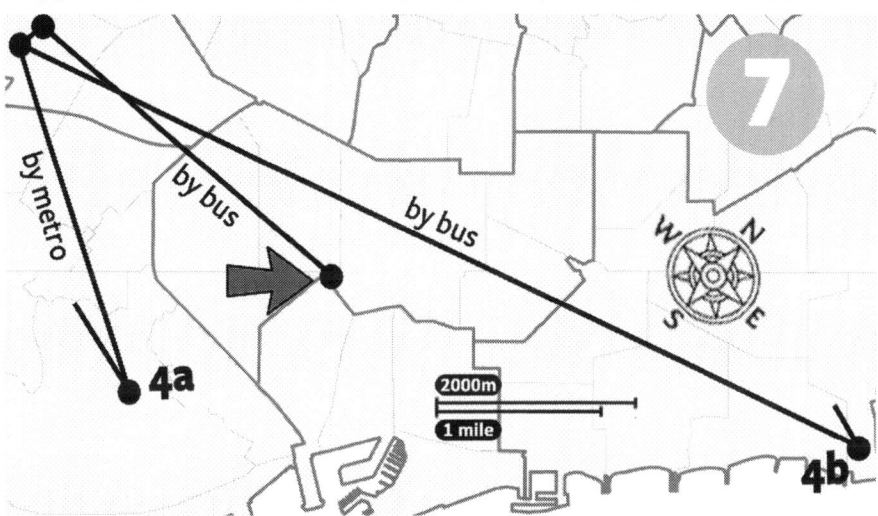

Nord. Get off at Arizala-Travessera de les Corts (15 stops, about 50'). From there, walk 5' to Camp Nou.

2. Camp Nou, FC Barcelona

The **Camp Nou** (see #41) is the football stadium of FC Barcelona ("Barça", pronounced '<u>bahr</u>-sah'), one of the local teams playing in La Liga, the top Spanish division, and one of the major actors in international football. The Camp Nou complex includes the stadium, the museum, an ice rink, the mini-stadium –where the younger sections play- a basketball court, and La Masia, the former football school of Barça players. The "Camp Nou Experience" tour provides a unique opportunity to visit the stadium and the museum. Expect to queue, especially during summer months, but the visit is worth!. Don't forget to get your season jersey.

3. Pista de Gel del Barça

Since you're already in the Camp Nou complex, you might want to have a bit of fun visiting the **Pista de Gel del Barça** (see #42), an ice rink where you can demonstrate your abilities skating on ice. Except in August, the rink is open all year round. You can, of course, rent all the necessary equipment there. After this activity, I propose to choose among these: visiting the Olympic Stadium Complex in Montjuïc hill or else the Bosc Urbà in Diagonal Mar -the opposite side of town.

4a. Olympic Stadium Complex

The **Olympic Stadium Complex** (see #33) is located in the Montjuïc hill, west of Barcelona. It includes the Olympic Stadium, and next to it the Palau Sant Jordi –basketball court and scenario of rock concerts - and the Olympic Museum. It's located in an area full of other attractions to see, like the MNAC or the Ethnology museums or the **Poble Espanyol** (see #32) among others.

or by metro+tram. Check their schedule as it varies across the year.

Dinner/snack

If you've chosen to go to the Barcelona Bosc Urbà attraction, you are next to the Diagonal Mar Shopping Centre which has plenty of restaurants and fast-food places to grab a bite. There's a wide range of options: tapas Basc-style, exotic all-you-can-eat, all kind of sandwich-and-sausages, Mexican, American and Far Eastern restaurants, etc. Take your pick! •

4b. Bosc Urbà

If you've chosen zip wires and hanging platforms instead , let's cross the city to get to the Fòrum area, where the **Barcelona Bosc Urbà** (*see #25*) attraction is located, an adventure park for kids with zip wires, hanging platforms and bungee jumping. The fastest way to get there is by metro

• •

A VIEW OF DOWNTOWN BARCELONA FROM THE MAREMAGNUM SHOPPING CENTER

TAPAS

Esqueixat de bacallà

- Salt cod, pepper, onion and black olive salad

Xai del Pirineus al forn amb romaní i fasigola

- Slow roasted mountain lamb with rosemary & thyme

The **best**...

page 174

to have a quick **bite**

for a sweet **treat**

page 176

specialty **shops**

page 178

The**best**...

Barcelona's got some great restaurants. Families visiting the city have so many options for eating, it can be overwhelming. There's no reason to eat at a chain restaurant you can find at home when you're in a city with so many great places that can easily accommodate kids with tasty and easy to eat kid-friendly food.

LA LLAVOR DELS ORIGENS

A treasure chest of Catalan regional products and 'tapas'

Away from the touristy tapas bars, Origens is a space for true Catalan gastronomy. A concept that evocates the tradition of the old cellars, so alive historically in villages and neighbourhoods in our towns; where at affordable prices, and at ease you can buy, eat and get to know our tradition. Their website is a wealth of information on Catalan cuisine. Finger licking good! •

[Zone: CENTRAL]
Passeig del Born, 4
Tel. +34 932 956 690
www.lallavordelsorigens.com

MERENDERO CAMPECHANO

G enuine barbeque-style restaurant in the heart of the city

Decorated with various elements reminiscent of the early modernist picnic areas on the outskirts of the city. The grill is the specialty of the house. Try the *embutits* –hashed meat sausages generally pork, seasoned with aromatic herbs or spices– on a *torrada* –a giant loaf of farmhouse toasted brown bread. And if you like meat this is your place: chicken, sausages, loin, roast pork...•

[Zone: CENTRAL]
València, 286
Tel. +34 932 156 233
campechanobarcelona.com

for fussy eaters

ZONE CENTRAL: HARD ROCK CAFE (Pl. Catalunya, 21, +34 932 702 305) the Barcelona branch of this famous chain — **LA FLAUTA** (Aribau, 23, +34 933 237 038) Mediterranean *tapas* — **EL NOU DE GRANADOS** (Enric Granados, 9, +34 933 300 303) more *tapas* — **TERESA CARLES** (Jovellanos, 2, +34 933 171 829) the best vegan breakfast and brunches — **KAPADOKYA** (Fus- teria, 6, +933 190 387) probably the best kebab — **LE PAIN QUOTIDIEN** (Provença, 300, +34 934 675 266) simply delicious organic brunches — **PIAZZE D'ITALIA** (Casanova, 94, +34 933 235 977) pasta e pizza, presto! — **ELS 4 GATS** (Montsió, 3, +34 933 024 140) plenty of atmos- phere in this rebuilt restaurant that was Picasso's old haunt • **ZONE EAST: LOS POLLOS DE LLULL** (Nàpols, 272, +34 931 622 250) great value for money chicken and chips — **TASCA I VINS**

tohaveaquick**bite**

ÁNDELE

MEATPACKING BISTRO

VIENA

A cheerful and colourful typical Mexican restaurant

It has also a grocery store where you can buy prepared food ready to go. For me, the best dishes are: the *torta de pollo* -a sort of chicken sandwich, cheese, beans, lettuce and onion-, the *enchilada verde* (very hot), tacos, and of course, cheese nachos. At first when you see the menu it seems a little bit expensive but the food rations are quite plentiful, so it's a great value for money ●

B ringing a little bit of New York spirit to Barcelona

An exact replica of an upscale New York Bistro, as if you were in the famous Manhattan neighbourhood. All the way down to the authentic serving aprons the wait staff wear, they don't miss even one detail. Homemade organic burgers, healthy salads, corn cob, brownies and delicious carrot cake are served. It's quite trendy, prepare to line up, especially in the evenings ●

S andwiches, sandwiches, and more sandwiches

A restaurant chain specialized in sandwiches: over 10 different types of German sausages, ham, roasted pork loin, bacon, cheese, chicken, vegetarian... teens love sandwiches! In 2006, a New York Times food critic called the *Ibèric* at Viena –a thin bread "flute" of Ibèric ham anointed with tomato squeezings- the best sandwich he's ever eaten. This is quality fast food ●

[Zone: NORTH-WEST]
Av. Diagonal 557 (mall center)
Tel. +34 933 211 017
www.andele.es

[Zone: NORTH-WEST]
Travessera de Gràcia 50-52
Tel. +34 932 008 908
www.meatpackingbistro.com

[Zone: CENTRAL]
Pelai, 16 (close to La Rambla)
Tel. +34 932 008 908
www.viena.es

● ●

(Indústria, 118 , +34 934 355 052) barbeque-style restaurant ● **ZONE WEST: LA TRAJINERA** (Gran Via de les Corts Catalanes, 459 , +34 934 265 394) the authentic Mexican experience in town — **SHANGAI 1930** (Buenos Aires, 11, +34 933 634 370) fine Chinese cuisine ● **ZONE NORTH-EAST: KIBUKA** (Goya, 9, +34 932 378 994) a superb Japanese with Brazilian inspiration — **MI GRACIA** (Encarnació, 52, +34 932 139 437) a cozzy and romantic Argentinian hideout ● **ZONE NORTH-WEST: LA TAGLIATELLA** (Muntaner, 359, +34 933 620 384) more fine Italian food — **ASADOR DE ARANDA** (Avinguda del Tibidabo, 31, +34 934 170 115) upscale braserie in a magnificent location ●

The**best**...

CAELUM

XOCOLATERIA LA NENA

I understand the importance for a little daily luxury. So to help everyone achieve this I've created this list of places where to eat a sweet treat in Barcelona. Sweets are the best reward for kids, isn't it so?

Desperate for candy? Check Happy Pills' jars filled with sugary treats and jelly hearts at carrer dels Arcs, 6 near Portal de L'Àngel .

Y**ou don't find many tea rooms serving delightful patisseries**

Caelum in Latin means heaven and this is just what Caelum is. Caelum is an unexpected find in the heart of the Barri Gòtic –located in the old medieval Jews baths, you've got to check the dowstairs level, it's simply amazing. The bakery has jams and treats all made by monks or nuns around Spain. This is a great place to find a unique gift to take home with you •

[Zone: CENTRAL]
Palla, 8 (near the Cathedral)
Tel. +34 933 026 993
www.caelumbarcelona.com

A**really special place for home made cakes, chocolate and dairy products**

Indulge in cups of rich hot chocolate –called *suïssos*– served with a plate of heavy homemade whipped cream and *melindros* –spongy sweet biscuits. The place, located in the cozy neighbourhood of Gràcia, is strewn with books and the area out back is designed to keep kids busy, making it an ideal family rest stop •

[Zone: NORTH-EAST]
Ramon i Cajal, 36
Tel. +34 932 851 476
Check their group in Facebook

ZONE CENTRAL: THINK-SWEET (Rambla Catalunya, 124) great homely cakes — **CUP & CAKE** (Enric Granados, 145) 100% hand-made cupcakes — **LA PALLARESA** (Petritxol, 11, +34 933 022 036) the best hot chocolate with *xurros* — **DULCINEA** (Petritxol, 2, +34 933 026 824) delicious sugary *ensaimades* — **BUENAS MIGAS** (Baixada de Santa Clara, 2, +34 933 191 380) try their cheese cake with peach! — **GRANJA VIADER** (Xuclà, 4) a mecca for lovers of rich, milky drinks — **AMORINO*** (Portaferrissa, 7) the cuttest ice-cream cones — **LA GRANJA** (Banys Nous, 4) another great place for chocolate with *xurros* — **CACAO SAMPAKA*** (Consell de Cent, 292) a shop with more than 100 varieties of chocolate — **XOCOA*** (Princesa, 10) bonbon and couture chocolates paradise! • **ZONE EAST: MARISA** (Gran de Sant Andreu, 241, +34 933 118 754) serving traditional homemade Catalan *pâtisserie* — **FARGGI** (Marina, 16) 'the' chain

for a sweet **treat**

CRÊPERIE ANNAÍCK

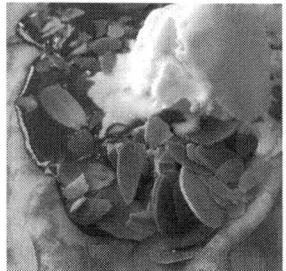

Fabulously eccentric *crêperie* with exceptional typical French pancakes

Located amidst a restored double-decker and old cinema seats and filled with a wondrous melée of one-off flea market finds. Their *crêpes* are unique: sweet or savoury, you'll find a filling to satisfy your craving. I recommend the *croque bretonne* –ham, cheese and egg– and the delicious *l'île Houat* – banana, chocolate and vanilla. Simply delicious! •

[Zone: EAST]
Ramon Trias Fargas, 2-4
Tel. +34 932 211 599
www.creperiebretonne.com

CASA DANONE

The Casa Danone is the world famous yogurt company's first restaurant

Danone's first restaurant and it was established for the occasion of Danone's 90th birthday in 2009. At their yogurt bar you can create your own and personal yogurt (frozen or not) with different toppings and flavors. Casa Danone offers as well a great, healthy, and very affordable menu that is inspired by Mediterranean cuisine •

[Zone: NORTH-WEST]
Av. Diagonal, 477
Tel. +34 934 109 092
www.danone.es

CORNELIA & CO.

Naturally healthy and delicious: a place where organic meet Barcelona

Take a seat at this 'Daily Picnic Store' any day of the week and let the sweet bakery scents whet your appetite; for brunch –a light pasta dish, a salad...– head there on Sunday mornings. A great place to drop in for a bite and drink or to pick up a beautifully packaged food gift, stop by on the way to bigger things or as a destination in itself •

[Zone: CENTRAL]
València, 225
Tel. +34 932 723 956
www.corneliaandco.com

• •

of ice-cream shops in town • **ZONE WEST: ENRIC ROVIRA*** (Josep Tarradellas, 113) have a *bombola* -chocolate-covered peppercorns, fried corn or pork rinds — **NATCHA** (Avinguda de Sarrià, 45 , +34 934 301 070) sofisticated *pâtisserie* • **ZONE NORTH-EAST: BUENAS MIGAS** (Passeig de Gràcia, 120, +34 932 385 549) pastries, tarts and cakes — **BODEVICI*** (Astúries, 2) healthy organic frozen yogurts • **ZONE NORTH-WEST: FOIX DE SARRIÀ*** (Plaça de Sarrià, 12) the *bourgeois pâtisserie* up town — **MONT-RODON*** (Travessera de les Corts, 269) good *sachers* and apple *strudels* •

* these are just stores

The**best**...

It's virtually impossible to list all the curious specialty shops that you'll find in Barcelona many of which hide behind unassuming façades in small streets across the city. I'd like to give you a glimpse, just a glimpse of some of those little gems but it's up to you to discover the rest. Just walk around the city and you might find them.

VINÇON

A great retro design and gadget shop in the most amazing building

Vinçon is the best design emporium in the city, with 10,000 products –everything from household items to the latest gadgets. Its mission is to purvey good design, period. Housed in the former home of artist Ramon Casas the showroom is filled with just anything you want which looks cool. The creative window displays alone are worth the trek, expect anything •

[Zone: CENTRAL]
Passeig de Gràcia, 96
Tel. +34 932 156 050
www.vincon.com

PAPABUBBLE

Papabubble, a quiet and unassuming candy shop, making it easy to miss

It's unconventional appearance makes it even harder to distinguish, it's more like a bizarre fusion of a futuristic kitchen and a mad scientist's lab. Their love for experimentation means you can witness their candy–making with all your senses: the smell of melting sugar, the mix of colours, the taste of the sweet. Excitement and high doses of imagination •

[Zone: CENTRAL]
Ample, 28 (in the Barri Gòtic)
Tel. +34 932 688 625
www.papabubble.com

ZONE CENTRAL: LA BASÍLICA GALERIA (Sant Sever, 7, +933 042 047) the most amazing jewelry I've ever seen — **EL REI DE LA MÀGIA** (Princesa, 11, +933 193 920) magic shop for magicians — **EL INGENIO** (Rauric, 6, +34 933 177 138) specialises in the production Of Catalan festival masks — **ALTAIR** (Gran Via, 616, +34 933 427 171) one of the biggest travel bookstores in the World — **SOMBRERERIA OBACH** (Call, 2, +34 933 184 094) no frills, just great hats since 1924 — **CASA** **GISPERT** (Sombrerers, 23, +34 933 197 535) toasting the best tasting nuts you'll ever have the pleasure to try — **TROIKA** (Unió, 3 bis) a true Russian supermarket— **LA MANUAL ALPAR-GATERA** (Avinyó, 7, +34 933 010 172) espadrilles, the ecological footwear made of natural material — **GANIVETERIA ROCA** (Plaça del Pí, 3, +34 933 021 241) has been furnishing Barcelona with knives, scissors, razors and every other imaginable cutting device — **HORITZONS** (València,

& most curious specialtyshops

ARLEQUÍ MASKS

Arlequí masks are the pinnacle of mystery, beauty, and seduction

Nothing catches the imagination as much as these works of art. Looking for an ornately decorated papier-mâché mask for a ball, masquerade ball, or a party? The walls here are dripping with masks, more than 200 different types, crafted from papier mâché and leather. Other trinkets and toys include finger puppets, mirrors and ornamental boxes •

[Zone: CENTRAL]
Princesa, 7 (in the Barri Gòtic)
Tel. +34 932 682 752
www.arlequimask.com

CASA PALAU

A word of creative flair and an appreciation for incredible detail

Since 1935, Palau has been supplying scale model enthusiasts with fine scale replicas of the most famous ships, trains and any other type of vehicle you might think of. All you need for scale modelling hobby is in this shop: model vintage cars; RC planes and helicopters; wooden model ships, and trains, lots of trains and all the terrain you might need for them •

[Zone: CENTRAL]
Pelai, 34 (near Pl.Catalunya)
Tel. +34 933 173 678
www.palauhobby.net

BARÇA STORE

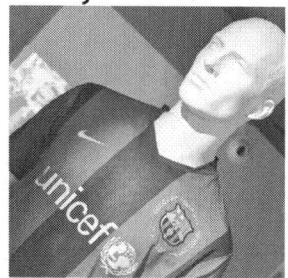

Get your very own Barça shirt with your name and the number of your idol

FCBotiga, the official club store, boasts 2000 m² of retail space in the Nou Camp Stadium filled with more than 3000 different articles, a 'showtime' section, where superimposed photographs of you with the players can be produced and purchased and an area called the 'Museum corner' which offers replicas of items on display in the museum •

[Zone: NORTH-WEST]
Inside FC Barcelona's stadium
Tel. +34 934 963 600
www.fcbarcelona.com

149, +34 934 513 097) the mountaineers' bookstore — **CORBETO'S BOOTS** (La Rambla, 40, +34 933 020 642) a cowboy's footware paradise — **ANAMORFOSIS** (Baixada de Santa Eulàlia, 4, +34 933 012 943) vintage scientific instruments • **ZONE EAST: FERRETERIA LLANZA** (Passeig de Sant Joan, 61, +34 932 656 469) a hardware store keeping everything as it was when opened in 1928 • **ZONE WEST: CERABELLA** (Comte Borrell, 41, +34 934 429 328) candle-making at its best • **ZONE NORTH-EAST: EQUIVALENZA** (Milton, 1) fragances and perfumes at affordable prices — **CASA ANITA** (Vic, 14, +34 932 376 002) a bookstore specialized in kids' books — **VOM FASS** (Cigne, 14, +34 934 16 06 73) a world of olive oils and vinegars •

so little space... and so much to say!

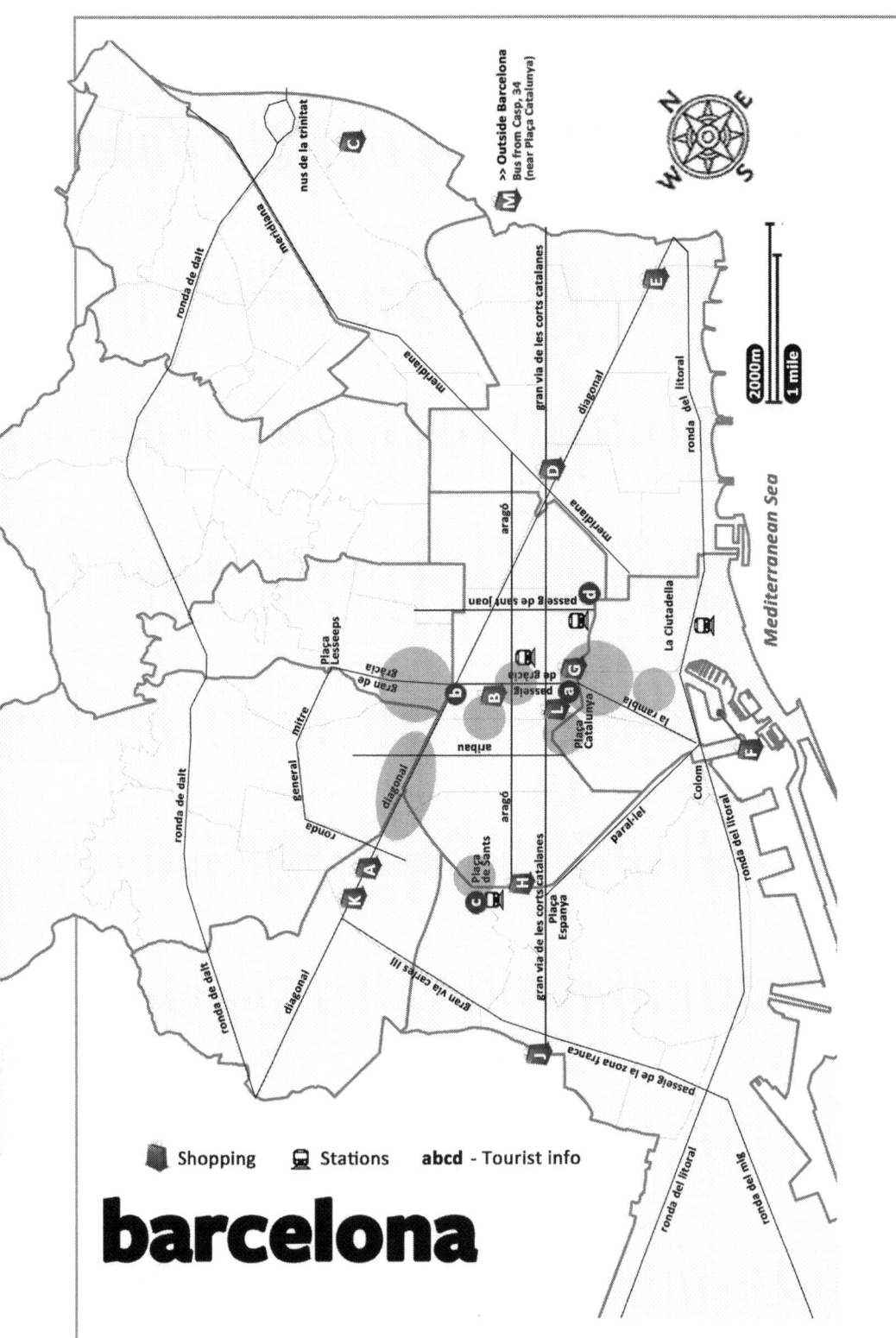

barcelona

🛍 Shopping 🚉 Stations **abcd** - Tourist info

Shopping
time!

If you love to shop then you're going to love Barcelona! Barcelona shopping offers over 30,000 shops and it is amongst Europe's top cities for fashion where you can find most of the mainstream stores and no shortage of designer outlets.

Barcelona is taking over that coveted space in shopaholics' hearts. With a heady mixture of unique boutiques, second-hand shops, flea markets, luxury shopping, malls and outlets, Barcelona has something for every kind of shopper. Characterized by originality and relative affordability, shopping in **Barcelona** has developed into a jubilant fashion, design, craft, and gourmet-food fair. The fact that different parts of town provide distinct contexts for shopping makes exploring the city and browsing boutiques inclusive activities.

Let me show you where are the main shopping areas of the city as well as the major malls and department stores •

Shop 'til you drop

"Centre"

This would be the area in the centre of Barcelona, west and south of the *Plaça Catalunya* and the streets to its southwest, at the Barri Gòtic, such as *Carrer Portal de l'Àngel, Carrer de la Portaferrissa, Carrer de la Boqueria*, and *Carrer de Ferran*, and around *Plaça de Sant Josep Oriol*. Here, the wide paved roads make way for winding little cobbled alleys. Every turn in this labyrinth leads to small stores tucked away in the corner with great deals or original products.

El Corte Inglés department store, spread over 9 floors and possibly the most important chain-store in Europe, can be found on the *Plaça de Catalunya*. Just opposite the square, **El Triangle** shopping mall hosts the biggest FNAC store in town as well as Sephora, the top shop in beauty products so there is no excuse not to always be looking your best!

To the west, next to El Triangle, you have *Carrer Pelai* full of fashion shops from the top brands such as Zara, Mango, Oysho, La Tienda de Lolín, Lefties -the outlet from Zara-, Blanco, Women's Secret, C&A, Punt Roma, Celio, Promod or Stradivarius among other as well as shoe stores like the famous Padeví, Scarpa, Noel, Scala Dei or Querol.

Also in the *Plaça Catalunya* you'll find the biggest Apple store in the south of Europe as well as the famous Hard Rock Café.

"Passeig de Gràcia"

If high-end is your middle name when it comes to purchases, *Passeig de Gràcia* is your place. A wide avenue that is the best place in town to find luxury brands. Have your platinum plastic at hand, ready to charge to the limit on this famous street. Visit the adjacent boulevard too, *Rambla de Catalunya*, it's worth it!

Scattered among luxury stores like Armani and Manolo Blahnik, check out modernist buildings like Gaudí's **La Pedrera** (*see #20*) and Casa Batlló. Post-shopping, eat at upscale bars and restaurants like Altinglao or Marenostrum. Don't forget to check out clothes and accessories from Spanish designers like Adolfo Dominguez and Roberto Verino while you're there.

"Diagonal"

At the end of *Passeig de Gràcia*, you'll find the longest avenue in Barcelona called *Avinguda Diagonal* or simply "*Diagonal*". Turn to your left, towards *Plaça Francesc Macià*. This is the place to look if you're after international fashion. Shops along here include Calvin Klein, Giorgio Armani, Gianni Versace and Gucci.

The city is also home to the famous so called **Shopping Line**. It stretches over 5km (3 miles) from the top of the Rambles, through Plaça de Catalunya along Passeig de Gràcia and up Avenue Diagonal. Much of the shopping line is pedestrianised making it a pleasant experience to wonder from shop to shop without worrying about traffic.

Along the Shopping Line you'll find a huge selection of shops including many of the big names like Tous, Loewe, Versace, Giorgio Armani, Carolina Herrera, Rabat, and Louis Vuitton, to name but a few but also many high quality local designer shops supplying a dizzy array of clothes, shoes, jewellery, apparel and accessories with chic European style •

Bargain-hunters should time their visits for the two annual sales. The winter sales start around 6 January until end of February and the summer sale lasts from late June to the end of August. Fantastic bargains can be had with generally up to 50% discount and sometimes 75% or more.

Upon reaching *Plaça Francesc Macià* you will find another **El Corte Inglés** department store, albeit smaller than the one in the *Plaça Catalunya*. Then continue walking on *Diagonal* towards *Plaça Maria Cristina*. On the way you'll find two of the most upscale shopping malls in the city: **L'Illa Diagonal** and **Pedralbes Centre**.

"Gràcia"

From the top of *Passeig de Gràcia*, where it crosses *Diagonal*, if you keep going north bound you'll reach the neighbourhood of *Gràcia*, a former village that was incorporated into Barcelona in the late 19th century. In *Gràcia*, search out creative and original wares for mind, body and home in the charming shops on *Carrer d'Asturies, Carrer Gran de Gràcia* and most especially *Carrer Verdi* . While in Gràcia, take the opportunity to have a sweet treat in **La Nena** (*see page 176*).

"Sants"

Next to Sants station, the main hub for trains in Barcelona -and the departing point for the airport bound trains- you have the neighbourhood of *Sants*, another bordering village that was absorbed into the current city of Barcelona in 1897.

The neighbourhood of *Sants* -much like *Gràcia*- has plenty of small, local shops, particularly along the *Carrer de Sants*, where you'll find shops selling shoes, low-end fashion, household goods, as well as all the essential groceries. For fresh produce, you've got the large **Hostafrancs** covered market, which is like a more orderly version of the famous **La Boqueria** market (*see #14*) just off *Les Rambles*. Offering everything from ham hocks to hake to honey dew melons, it's a good way to get some first-hand experience of a real Catalan shopping experience •

Malls and department stores

Barcelona has a vast number of shopping malls and department stores conveniently spread across the city. While they might vary in size, you'll find that most of them offer the majority of the top brands. It's also important to notice that in some shopping areas, such as around Portal de l'Àngel, Portaferrisa and Pelai in the central zone, you're bound to find almost all the brand stores as well lined up one next to the other.

El Corte Inglés is considered the quintessential department store in Spain and you'll find five or six of them in Barcelona •

A short trip from Barcelona city centre -about an hour- **La Roca Village** features over 100 outlets where both local and international brand-name items can be bought for up to 60% off the normal retail price all year round. It's a veritable retail village, with individual storefronts and restaurants linked by wide boulevards, so try to choose a nice day – you'll be spending some time outside.

• • • Shopping malls and department stores • • • • • • •

A L'ILLA DIAGONAL
Avinguda Diagonal, 557
Lat: 41.39021337
Long: 2.1357438
Tel +34 934 440 000
www.lilla.com
10:00-21:30 Mon-Sat

B BULEVAR ROSA
Passeig de Gràcia, 53
Lat: 41.39271
Long: 2.16407
Tel +34 932 158 331
www.bulevardrosa.com
10:30-21:00 Mon-Sat

C LA MAQUINISTA
Potosí, 2
Lat: 41.440732
Long: 2.198253
Tel +34 933 608 971
www.lamaquinista.com
10:00-22:00 Mon-Sat

D LES GLÒRIES
Diagonal, 208
Lat: 41.405111
Long: 2.190597
Tel +34 934 860 404
www.lesglories.com
10:00-22:00 Mon-Sat

E DIAGONAL MAR CENTRE
Diagonal, 3
Lat: 41.410442
Long: 2.216233
Tel 902 530 300
www.diagonalmarcentre.es
10:00-22:00 Mon-Sat

F MAREMAGNUM
Moll d'Espanya, 5
Lat: 41.37737
Long: 2.18331
Tel +34 932 258 100
www.maremagnum.es
10:00-22:00 Mon-Sun

Opening hours

Most shopping malls, outlets and large stores are open from 10am to 9pm or later, Monday through Saturday. Only **Maremagnum** is open also on Sundays as it's located inside the harbour area where city regulations apply differently.

Smaller neighbourhood shops typically open from 10am to 2pm, close for lunch for a few hours, and re-open after 4pm for four more hours Monday through Friday, and are open reduced hours Saturdays.

Stores accept cash, and most credit or debit cards (VISA, Mastercard and Maestro among others) with proper I.D. for payment. Personal and business cheques, American Express and Discover credit cards are not widely accepted ●

See map on page 180

(G) EL CORTE INGLÉS
Plaça de Catalunya, 14
Lat: 41.38835
Long: 2.17003
Tel +34 933 063 800
www.elcorteingles.es
9:30-21:30 Mon-Sat

(H) LES ARENES
Gran Via de les Corts Catalanes 373
Lat: 41.3763
Long: 2.149006
Tel +34 932 890 244
www.arenasdebarcelona.com
10:00-22:00 Mon-Sat

(J) GRAN VIA 2
Avinguda de la Gran Via, 75
(L'Hospitalet)
Lat: 41.35969
Long: 2.12871
Tel +34 932 590 522
www.granvia2.com
10:00-22:00 Mon-Sat

(K) PEDRALBES CENTRE
Diagonal, 609
Lat: 41.3888
Long: 2.1286
Tel +34 934 106 821
www.pedralbescentre.com
10:00-21:00 Mon-Sat

(L) EL TRIANGLE
Plaça Catalunya, 1
Lat: 41.38628
Long: 2.16941
Tel +34 933 180 108
www.eltriangle.es
10:00-22:00 Mon-Sat

(M) LA ROCA VILLAGE
Santa Agnès de Malanyanes
(La Roca del Vallès)
Lat: 41.61114
Long: 2.34373
Tel +34 938 423 939
www.larocavillage.com
10:00-22:00 Mon-Sat

Comparing **prices**

(A) Pair of jeans (Levis 501 or similar)
(B) Summer dress in a chain store (Zara...)
(C) Pair of Nike shoes
(D) Pair of men leather shoes

	(A)	(B)	(C)	(D)
AMSTERDAM	80.16	40.00	89.50	110.00
AUCKLAND	60.83	46.08	92.17	104.46
ATHENS	90.00	35.00	90.00	90.00
BEIJING	102.08	51.04	102.08	114.84
BERLIN	80.00	35.00	74.00	120.00
BERN	80.41	38.20	84.03	96.09
BRUSSELS	80.00	50.00	85.00	100.00
DUBLIN	70.00	40.00	75.00	70.00
CAPE TOWN	46.84	27.32	54.65	54.65
CHICAGO	37.56	27.38	75.89	70.42
COPENHAGEN	107.26	46.92	107.26	107.26
HAMBURG	70.00	45.00	99.50	75.00
HELSINKI	97.00	32.50	100.00	90.00
EDINBURGH	69.79	40.71	69.79	69.79
JOHANNESBURG	55.38	31.23	62.45	54.65
KIEV	67.13	47.95	78.26	95.89
LISBON	80.00	30.00	80.00	80.00
LJUBLJANA	80.00	30.00	80.00	80.00
LONDON	69.79	34.90	69.79	69.79
LOS ANGELES	37.16	33.25	62.59	78.24
MADRID	90.00	35.00	80.00	90.00
MANCHESTER	52.35	34.90	63.98	58.16
MELBOURNE	71.80	57.44	107.70	107.70
MILAN	90.00	30.00	80.00	120.00
MOSCOW	83.00	59.29	83.00	118.57
NEW YORK	41.08	31.30	62.59	62.59
OTTAWA	44.60	22.30	74.33	70.61
PARIS	92.50	30.00	85.00	120.00
PRAGUE	73.50	38.61	77.37	65.77
QUEBEC CITY	32.33	29.73	68.92	83.62
ROME	95.00	40.00	105.00	95.00
SEATTLE	37.16	31.30	70.42	78.24
SHANGHAI	102.08	41.47	114.84	102.08
STOCKHOLM	120.36	37.43	103.66	138.22
SYDNEY	75.39	61.03	107.70	107.70
TOKYO	61.88	52.21	77.35	77.35
TORONTO	42.15	29.73	85.48	83.58
VIENNA	90.00	34.50	75.00	80.00
WARSAW	69.40	37.01	69.40	69.40
BARCELONA	80.00	30.00	80.00	80.00

All prices shown have been converted to EUROS (€) for easy comparison.

Whatto **buy**

+D CONTI
7 CAMICIE
ADOLFO
DOMINGUEZ
AITA
ALAIN AFFLELOU
ALDO
AMY GEE
ANTONIO MIRÓ
ANTONY
MORATO
ARISTOCRAZY
ARMANI OUTLET
BALLY
BARBOUR
BDBA
BECARA
BELSTAFF
BERSHKA
BIBA
BILLABONG
BIMBA & LOLA
BODUM
BONPOINT
BOSTON
BROWNIE
BULGARI
BURBERRY
CALVIN KLEIN
CALZEDONIA
CAMPER
CARHARTT
CAROLINA HER-
RERA
CASAS
CASTAÑER
CHANGE
CHANTELLE
CLAIRE'S
CLARKS
CELIO
COACH
CÓDIGO BÁSICO
COLUMBIA
CONTI
COOKED IN
BARCELONA
CORTEFIEL

COTTET
CUSTO
DC STORE
DESIGUAL
DI PREGO
CAMICIE
DIESEL
DOCKERS
DOTZE DE CORS
DOUGLAS
ELENA MIRÓ
ESCADA
ESE O ESE

ESUAP
ETAM LINGERIE
ETXART &
PANNO
FOLLI FOLLIE
FOOT LOCKER
FOREVER 21
FUREST
G-STAR RAW
GANT
GEORGES RECH

GEOX
GUESS
H&M
HACKETT
HAVAIANAS
HILFIGER DENIM
HOLLISTER
HOSS INTROPIA
HUGO BOSS
HUNKEMÖLLER
HUSH PUPPIES
IKKS WOMEN
INSIDE

INTIMISSIMI
JACK & JONES
JAVIER SIMORRA
KAOTIKO
KOROSHI
KUROKAI
LA PERLA
LACOSTE
LEONCE
LEVI'S
LYNE'S

LOEWE
LOTUSSE
LUSH
MACSON
MANDARINA
DUCK
MANGO
MARYPAZ
MASSIMO DUTTI
MAYDO
MBT
MCQUINN
MISAKO

MISS SIXTY
MUNICH
NEKANE
NICE THINGS
NIKE STORE
NO PROBLEM
ORANGE
OYSHO
PANAMA JACK
PEDRO DEL
HIERRO

PEPE JEANS
PERFUMERIA
JULIA
PIMKIE
PODIUM
PRIMARK
PROMOD
PULL AND BEAR
PUNTO BLANCO
QUEROL
RIP CURL
RITUALS
ROBERTO
VERINO
SABON
SALSA
SAN MARINA
SEBAGO
SFERA
SHANA
SISLEY
SITA MURT
SPAZIO
SPRINGFIELD
STRADIVARIUS
SUITEBLANCO
SUN FASHION
SUPERDRY
SUSUU
SYSTEM ACTION
TASCON
TCN
TEZENIS
THE BODY SHOP
TIMBERLAND
TOSCANA
TRUCCO
ULANKA
U-CASAS
UNO DE 50
VERSACE
VIALIS
VOGUE
WOMEN'S
SECRET
XTREM DE
CONTI
ZARA

got enough choice?

Discovery Hunt

by Gisel·la and me

Welcome to the **DISCOVERY HUNT** around the old city in Barcelona. You'll need to use your eyes and your brain to solve these challenges. Your hunt will take you to some of the most popular and famous sites in the old city, located in **Barri Gòtic** (pronounced "_bah-ree goh-teak_"). Whether you like art, science, history or just experimenting with new places, you'll find plenty to do there. Have fun on your hunt and good luck. You will have an absolutely exciting time exploring this great neighbourhood!

INSTRUCTIONS

1. Your **Discovery Hunt** adventure has many challenges for you to complete. It's been designed to be achieved at a comfortable pace but don't feel compelled to complete all the challenges in one day!

2. Write each response to the questions presented into the appropiate box. Make sure you double-check your answers as they might be needed for other challenges down the road. If your answers are incorrect you might not be able to complete the hunt.

3. If you get stuck you can check page 216 where you'll find the correct answers to the hunt. But be a sport and don't cheat!

1. Columbus monument

The **statue of Christopher Columbus** at the top of his monument, which cardinal point is it pointing to? •

2. How many lion figures surround the Columbus monument? •

Now, take the main boulevard in front of the lions, named La Rambla, and walk opposite to the sea, which, in Barcelona, means 'towards the mountain' as the locals call it, that is the Collserola hills where Tibidabo (*see #39*) is, north of the city.

3. On the opposite side of the boulevard you'll see a building with some letters in the façade. Some of them are 'missing'. Find out what's the full name of that building. Hint: it's an art centre •

Keep on walking on La Rambla. A few metres ahead, to your right, you'll find a white monument on top of which there's another statue –albeit this time a marble statue. This is Mr. Frederic Soler, a very famous playwright from the mid 1800s. Look at his head. Which way is he looking at? Follow it.

4. A bit further up, to your left, you'll find a curious building with many 'heads' –technically these are '*busts*'– in its façade. Take a picture •

Now we'll leave la Rambla for a minute to visit the Plaça Reial (Catalan for *Royal Plaza*). Find a small street to your right which will lead you to a big square with many arches.

5. Plaça Reial

The **Plaça Reial** (pronounced *plah-sah reh-ee-ahl*) has been for many centuries a main meeting point in the city. Nowadays it is crowded with tourists day and night as there are many restaurants, bars and clubs. Don't miss the elaborate patterns of the lanterns surrounding the square. They were designed by Gaudí. The shield you'll see in some of them is the coat of arms of the city of Barcelona. How many arches are there 'inside' this square? •

Return to La Rambla

6. The **Teatre del Liceu** (pronounced *lee-seh-oo*) is an opera house built in 1847 which has seen the world's most famous opera singers and plays being performed there. To find it you'll have to look for a building with a huge clock on its façade as well as several flags. Then tick this •

Move on, continue walking La Rambla

7. Look for a building with some exotic far-eastern drawings in its façade. It also has some umbrellas and, right at the corner of the building you'll see also a dragon. Next to it there's a very small square with a fountain with three spouts. What's the name of the square? Hint: it shares its name with a very, very famous food market, which by the way, it's located only a few metres away •

From here, we'll head towards the 'centre of power' of Catalonia, the Plaça Sant Jaume, where La Generalitat (the equivalent to the White House in Washington, or 10 Downing Street in London) and the Barcelona City Hall are located. To get there, take the street closer to the fountain with the three spouts (Boqueria Street). Some 150 metres ahead you'll find a shop that sells hats and berets. Its name is Obach, a typical Catalan lastname. Keep on straight.

8. We've reached now the **Plaça Sant Jaume** (or *Saint James Square* in English). Two impressive buildings are at either side of the square, one is La Generalitat where the president of Catalonia and its cabinet work and the other one is the City Hall, where the mayor and its team work. Can you correctly identify them? Don't guess, investigate on your own and ask if necessary. The guards at the doors of each building will happily help you. On the Generalitat these are the Mossos d'Esquadra, the Catalan national police, on the City Hall these are the Guardia Urbana, or city police. Which building is at your left? And at your right? •

Now we'll head to the Plaça del Rei –or the King's Square, not to be confused with Plaça Reial which we saw earlier. This square has seen also its share of historical events albeit its finest hours were prior to the 15th century. In this square, King Ferdinand of Aragon was hurt in an attempt on his life in 1492 and legend says that one can still see three royal blood droplets on the third stair of the staircase to the Saint Agatha Chapel. To get to Plaça del Rei, take Llibreteria street (look around Plaça Sant Jaume to see which one is this street). Once you've found it, take it and you'll have to pass "as many streets" as the answer you gave in question 1 before turning to your left. So if you said 2, walk pass two streets and turn left on the third one, if you said 3… well, you know the drill!.

9. If you counted correctly on question 1, you should now be seeing a 'tall' building with many arches. That's **King Martin Watchtower**, one of the tallest buildings in Europe when built in 1421… but's merely five stories tall… a bit ridiculous nowadays, isn't it? Walk towards the square, find the staircase and see if you can confirm the legend of the royal blood droplets. Are they really there? In this square you'll also find a

glass door, during the Middle Ages that used to be where the 'executioner' lived… scary, eh? Have a picture taken while standing in front of the door •

Now try to spot this tile (*see picture*), which is located on the wall of one of the buildings in the square. It's a knight in armour on his horse. Which way is he looking?. Walk that way and take the first street to your right, it's a small narrow and a bit uphill passage. At the end you'll reach the back of a cathedral. To make sure you're on the right track, look up: is there a unicorn statue? If so, you're all right. Take the street to your right, it has some blue colour tiles similar to the one you've seen before, not a knight though.

In front of you there's a big square now, use the stairs in the middle or the ramp on the right. Walk towards the middle of the square. From there you'll be able to best appreciate the impressive cathedral, it's called Saint Eulàlia's Cathedral to be precise, and she's co-patron saint of the city. If you look left, in the distance you'll see a building with a bright wave-like roof. Its colours remind those of a traffic light: red, yellow and green. Take that direction.

10. After a while the street widens a bit, there's a huge riveted door to your left –this is a side entrance to the cathedral. Keep on walking. A few metres before reaching the end of this street, where the big square and the main entrance to the Cathedral are, check the wall to your left. In one of the stones almost at ground level there's a very old medieval inscription (like a modern graffiti!), what does it say? Hint: it's one word only, five letters •

11. You're now at the **Mercat de Santa Caterina** (pronounced *mer-cat dah sahn-tah cah-tah-ree-nah*), a food market where you can find all kind of meat, vegetables, fish, fruit and even exotic food. Years ago there was this stall where you could buy caramelized ants and scorpions (gross!... but delicious I got to admit) but it seems this far-eastern 'trend' didn't catch on with the locals. Have a picture taken showing the colourful façade of the market •

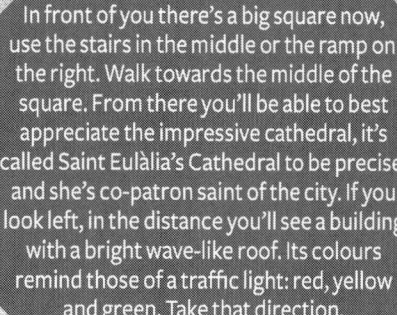

Now, let's walk back to the main street we just crossed when coming from the Cathedral: Via Laietana. Then take your left and walk this busy street for 100 meters or so. You'll reach a small square, greet the knight on the bronze horse, his name is Ramon Berenguer III 'El Gran' (*the Great*), count of many territories in Catalonia between 1082 and 1131 and one of the best generals the Catalans have ever had. Around the year 1125, he became a knight of the Order of the Temple –like the one in the *Indiana Jones and the Last Crusade* movie!

12. Keep on walking and 50 metres later you'll reach **Plaça Angel**. Find the press kiosk and take the street next to it, it's called **Argenteria** (meaning *silver* in Catalan, evolved from the Latin word *argentum*). After 350 metres (385 yards), or 5' walk, you'll find yet another square normally full of people having coffee or a drink on the street terraces –unless it's raining, of course!– and with a church to your left: **Santa Maria del Mar**. Face its main façade and look high above the door. During a (rare) earthquake occurred in Barcelona in 1428, the enormous rose window fell and killed some 30 parishioners. It was rebuilt in 1459. All right, this is the main entrance, but how many entrances are there in total (counting this one that is)? •

Let's go back to the main door of the church, look at both sides, take the street to your right. You can immediately see a torch high above a red semi arch in the middle of the street.

13. This is the 'eternal flame' of the **Fossar de les Moreres**, a memorial plaza to the fallen Catalans of the war of 1714 in which the Spanish and French troops invaded Catalonia. In this square there are buried the defenders of the city that died during the Siege of Barcelona. Every **September 11th**, the national day of Catalonia, Catalans pay homage to those heroes. There's a poem written in four languages in the red semi arch, can you tell me the **11th** word on the English version of the poem? •

14. Follow straight and look for a 'woman painted on a door with the same number of feet as days a week has'. Have your picture taken with her •

15. Once you've greeted the woman, check at your left -in the middle of the boulevard- a big metal trunk which sits on a bench. You can take a picture if you want •

16. Keep going, in front you'll see a large metal building. That's the **Mercat del Born** –born is the place where jousting took place during the Middle Ages. The Mercat del Born was the main wholesale food market in the city for nearly 100 years and was one of the first iron structures in Barcelona. But, in what year was it built? Hint: check the main façade, under the shield of the city •

17. When you've reached the main gate, turn your head to your right. At the end of the street there's a train station, the one in the picture, which one is it? •

18. Walk into the station, enter the hall and tell me how many big clocks are there on their walls •

19. Let's leave the station and walk towards your right. At 150 metres or so you'll see a dark metal gate with two statues at each side. That's the entrance to a very important public park in Barcelona. The zoo is there too. Which is its name? •

Walk towards the statue of a soldier on a horseback that seems to be looking at you. Then locate the back of a church –hint: check for a bell tower. It's very close! Walk towards the church. From there you'll see a white statue in the distance in front of a pond. Go there.

20. Now you're in front of the small pond, can you see the building behind it? what is it? Hint: check the huge word on its façade and, albeit it's in Catalan, you'll immediately recognize it since it's very similar to the English one •

21. Then take the pathway right to the black statue. After a 2' walk you'll find a loved landmark icon for every kid in town: a stone mamooth! Have your picture taken with him as a memento of your visit •

22. A few metres ahead there's a big monumental fountain. Check the golden quadriga –a chariot drawn by several horses. How many horses are there? •

23. Do you want to improve your luck in life? Come close to the edge of the fountain, turn around and flip a coin while thinking of a wish. Now, how many horses were there in the quadriga? Take that number and multiply it by 3. The result is the number of paces you'll have to walk forward. •

Turn your head to your right. Can you see some sort of a 'castle'? If not, perhaps you should walk a few more paces. Walk then towards that building –the 'castle'. When you've reached the main avenue, just before arriving at the 'castle', if you look again to your right you'll see a big arch at the distance. That's the finish line of this hunt.

25. Bravo! you have reached the arch now. Not as big as the one in Paris, but still impressive, isn't it? Remember those old movies depicting Roman exploits? Don't you feel a bit like those Roman generals returning home after a victorious campaign? Your last test: have someone taking your picture while standing underneath the arch making a V for Victory sign! •

24. But first, on your way towards the arch, just before reaching the park gates you'll see some lizard-like 'figures' on your left (actually they're dragons). How many are there? •

Continue now your race to the arch. The arch's name is Arc de Triomf (yes, triumph in English). This reddish brickwork arch in the Moorish Revival style was built for the 1888 Barcelona Universal Exhibition.

CONGRATULATIONS!

You've succesfully completed this Discovery Hunt. Me and Gisel·la –who designed this hunt– hope you've had a fun time.

Now, don't you think you deserve a treat? Just head for **LOLITA BAKERY** (Portal Nou, 20 - Tel +34 933 103676) which is literally a stone's throw from Arc de Triomf –less than 5' walk!– and get one of the best cupcakes you'll find in Barcelona.

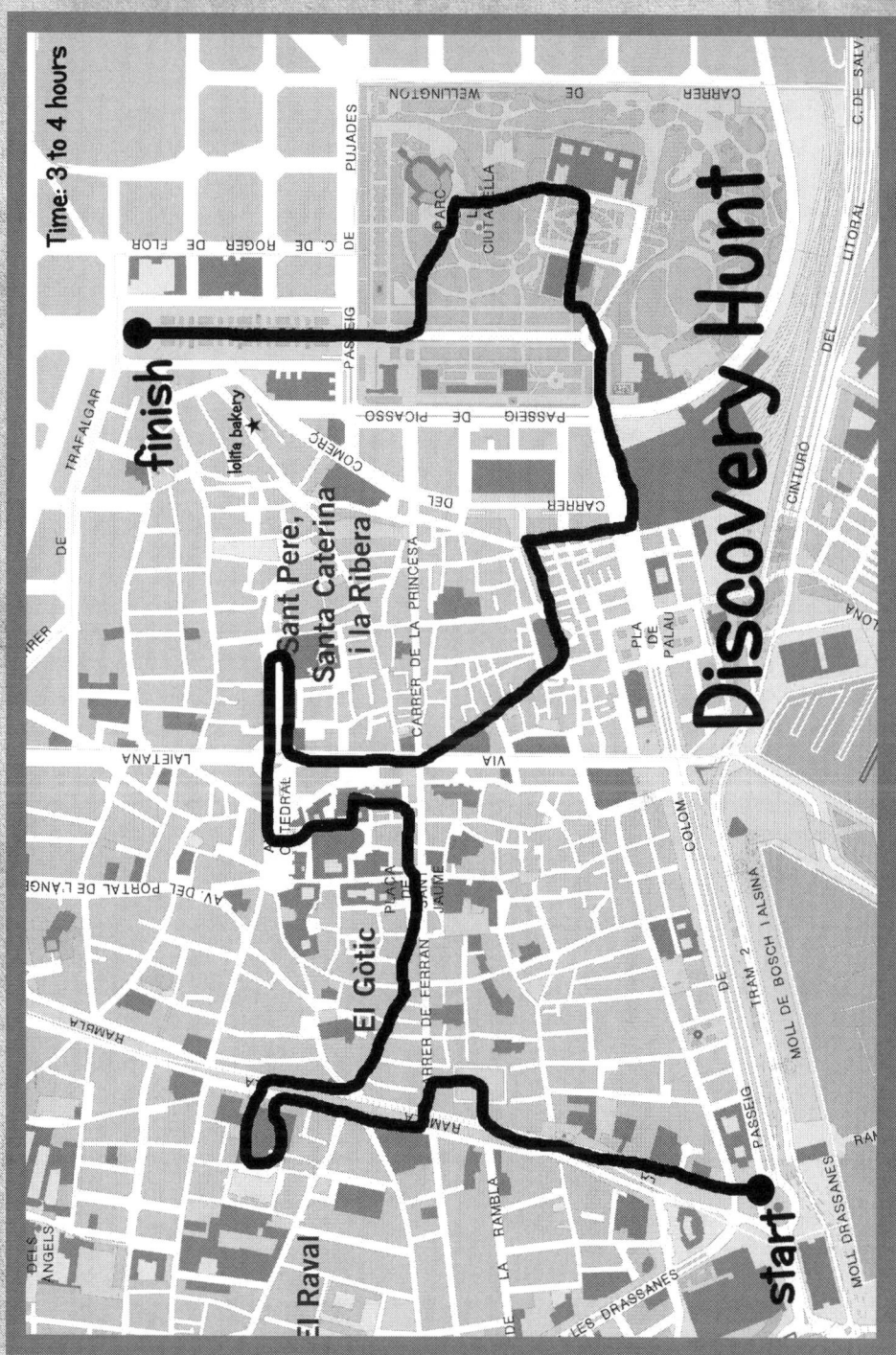

Time: 3 to 4 hours

Discovery Hunt

finish

start

Sant Pere, Santa Caterina i la Ribera

El Gòtic

El Raval

lolita bakery

195

It's good to **know**...

Travelling across the city

The cheapest and often fastest way to travel across the city is by using the public transport network. There are several types of transport passes but the most used is the **T-10 travel card** valid for 10 journeys. It's valid for metro, buses, tram (except Blue Tram) and FGC –which run train lines similar to the metro around the city centre– and RODALIES (the train network). The T10 is also valid on the RODALIES train to the airport but not valid on the AeroBus (the express bus service to the airport). For **zone 1** –covering all districts of the city of Barcelona–

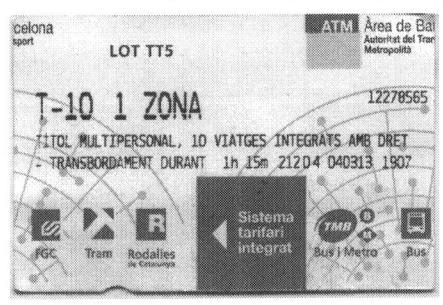

it cost around 10.-€. Compare it to a single ticket and you're saving 50% each time. The T-10 is multi-person so it can be used by more than one person (a family, for example). Each person using it must validate a journey by inserting the card into the machine. It's also intermodal which means it can be used

on more than one means of transport and all be counted as a single journey provided that your journey is less than 75 minutes. For example, you can make changes at metro stops (but don't leave the station), then leave the metro and jump on a bus to finish your journey or vice versa as long as the total length of the journey is less than 75 minutes.

Note that you can't re-enter the metro once you have left it - this would count as another journey. In any case, when using a T-10 you have to validate each time you board a different means of transport. But if you want free unlimited number of journeys on public transport for the duration of your holiday with discounts on activities consider the **Barcelona Card**. It can save you a lot of bother in buying tickets and save you some money. See the **Metropolitan Transport Authority** website (*www.tmb.cat*) for information •

Shop 'til you drop!

Shopping is available all day around (10am-10pm) in department stores and malls and until 9pm in most city centre shops. Smaller shops in the other districts might be closed between 2pm to 5pm but then they remain open until 8 or even 9 pm. Barcelona is famous for being one of Europe's fashion capitals so take this fantastic opportunity and *"shop 'til you drop!"*. Check page 181 •

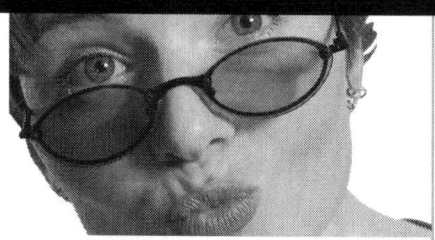

Sun, sun and sun

In Barcelona weather is quite mild in winter (8-12°C) and hot and wet in summer (30-33°C). It doesn't rain that much, mostly in Apr-May and in Sep-Oct... but when it does, it does! Don't worry though, they tend to be short downpours •

We Catalans are generally less guarded about personal space than people in Britain or the US. The common greeting between members of the opposite sex and between two women, even the first time that the two parties have met, is a kiss on both cheeks. Men greet each other by shaking hands •

Do not be angry with the rain; it simply does not know how to fall upwards

Vladimir Nabokov

Public holidays

As a general rule of thumb, many museums and some attractions are closed on Monday. Also, on certain public holidays, such as 25th and 26th December and 1st and 6th January among others. For more information check the attractions' websites or ask your receptionist at the hotel. Also, you can get more information at any Tourist Information Centre across the city •

Crime in Barcelona

IT'S MOSTLY A SAFE CITY BUT UNFORTUNATELY WE HAVE PICKPOCKETS, ESPECIALLY AROUND TOURIST ATTRACTIONS AND THE CITY CENTRE... SO BE ALERT AND WATCH YOUR BELONGINGS AT ALL TIMES. FOR INFO: WE HARDLY HAVE ANY GUN CRIME AT ALL •

Good manners

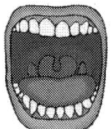

When you enter a shop or any other establishment it is polite to greet other people by saying *"Bon Dia"* -good morning in Catalan, the local language •

In Barcelona, lunch times are normally between noon and 3:30pm and dinners between 8:30pm and 11pm although you can find restaurants and bars serving food until past midnight, mostly on Fridays and Saturdays. My advice though is that you have lunch before 1:30pm because locals tend to lunch at around 2pm and most restaurants get very crowed, especially in the central districts of the city •

Eating out

It's good to **know**...

Until *dusk?*

In this guide you'll find often that an attraction is open "*until dusk*". Barcelona is a very luminous city and there is natural light until 9pm or more during summer while in winter dusk will come between 5 and 6pm •

Don't get (too) smart...

Contrary to appearances, Barcelonians have an advanced queuing culture. They may not stand in an orderly line, but they're normally very aware of when it's their turn, particularly at market stalls. The standard drill is to ask when you arrive, "*Quí és l'últim?*" (Who's last?, pronounced "*kee ehs looltc*eam"), and say "*jo*" (me, pronounced "*joh*") to the next person who asks. If you try to jump the queue you are likely to have someone biting your head off •

House numbering

As in most of Europe, the house numbering scheme is to number each plot on one side of the road with ascending odd numbers, from 1, and those on the other with ascending even numbers, from 2. Now you know! •

How to hail a taxi?

In Barcelona you can hail a taxi wherever it's convenient for you. Simply raise your arm when a taxi passes by. Make sure it has the green light on the roof lighted up, that means it's available. Note it won't stop if you are next to a taxi rank. Taxis in Barcelona are coloured in yellow (doors) and black, they are very easy to spot and there are more than 12000 of them so it should be easy to catch one when you need it •

Advantages for you

Check the online shop of **Barcelona Turisme** (*bcnshop. barcelonaturisme.com*) run by the City Hall, where you will find plenty of offers and discounts for many museums and visitor attractions as well as for transports and other venues •

Don't be surprised if people bump into you on the street or crowd or push past you on the bus or metro without apologising: it's not seen as rude. That does not mean you can go bumping into everybody, of course! •

Say a few
words in **Catalan**

Put away the Spanish dictionary mi amigo, because if you want to get along with the folk of Catalonia you'll find a few choice Catalan phrases a sharper weapon in your armoury of charm. Yes, we Barcelonians are very protective about our beloved Catalonia, which we regard as a separate country to Spain, and although you will get by just fine in Spanish you'll certainly pull away from the crowd with a few choice Catalan phrases up your sleeve.

But first a little introduction. Catalan is an entirely separate language to Spanish, and not just a separate dialect as many assume. It is spoken by around 10.5 million people, not only in Catalonia but also in Valencia and the Balearic Islands, in the small country of Andorra in the Pyrenees, in the Roussillon region of France and in the northwest Sardinian tiny city of Alghero (l'Alguer). For modern speakers, think of a mix of Spanish and French with a bit of Italian thrown in and you're half way there.

A word on genders… Catalan, as other languages like Spanish or French, has grammatical genders so some words vary whether you are referring to a male or a female. For example, in Catalan the word 'monkey' is '*mono*' if you're talking about a male and '*mona*' if it's a female. Note the change at the end of the word, '-a' instead of '-o'. Therefore, in the following list you will find a couple of variations in some sentences to be used either for a male or for a female. These are indicated by [him] and [her]. Use as appropiate.

Regarding pronounciation it's a bit like in English, every region has its own variations and the same word varies slightly from one to the next. Being myself a Barcelonian in the following list I've provided the *central Catalan* variation which contains sounds a bit more 'open' such as '*duh*', '*eh*' and '*oh*'. Try pronouncing them… •

Useful words

ENGLISH	CATALAN	It sounds like...
Hello	Hola	oh-lah
Good day	Bon dia	bohn dee-ah
How are you? (formal)	Com està?	com ehs-tah
How are you? (informal)	Què tal?	keh tahl
Very well	Molt bé	mohl beh
Not so good	Anar fent	ah-nah fen
Better	Millor	mee-yohr
Thank you	Gràcies	grah-see-uhs
You're welcome	De res	duh ress
Please	Si us plau	see yoos plow
Goodbye (bye)	Adeu	ah-deh-oo
Yes / No	Sí / No	see / noh
Excuse me (pardon me)	Disculpi (perdoni)	this-cool-pee (pahr-don-eem)
I'm sorry	Ho sento	oo sehn-two
Where is...?	On és...?	ohn ehs
To the left	Cap a l'esquerra	ahl ehs-keh-ra
To the right	Cap a la dreta	ah lah dreh-tah
How much is it?	Quant costa?	kwahnt cost-ah
I want...	Vull	boo-ee
I would like...	Voldria	vohl-dree-ah
Do you have...?	Té?	teh
When?	Quan?	kwan
What?	Què?	keh
Sure / of course	Segur / Clar que sí	seh-goo / klah kah see
Is there...?	Hi ha...?	ee ah
Yesterday	Ahir	ah-ee
Today	Avui	ah-boo-ee
Tomorrow	Demà	deh-mah
More	Més	mehss
Less	Menys	meh-nyus

and phrases

ENGLISH	CATALAN	*It sounds like...*
What time is it?	Quina hora és?	<u>kee</u>-nah <u>oh</u>-ra ehss
Let's go	Au, anem	owh, <u>ah</u>-nehm
What's your name (*formal*)	Cóm es diu vostè?	kom ass <u>dee</u>-oo boo-<u>steh</u>
What's your name (*informal*)	Cóm et dius?	kom at <u>dee</u>-oos
My name is...	Em dic...	am dick...
Nice to meet you	Encantat[encantada] de conèixer-te	an-cahn-<u>tat</u> [an-cahn-<u>tah</u>-dah] duh koo-<u>neh</u>-ee-shut
Same here / same to you	Igualment	ee-goo-<u>ahl</u>-men
Mister / Mrs **Miss**	Senyor / Senyora Senyoreta	se-<u>nior</u>/se-<u>nior</u>-ah se-nior-<u>eh</u>-tah
Where are you from?	D'ón ets?	don ehts
I'm from...	Sóc de...	sock duh...
How old are you? (*formal*)	Quants anys té?	kwans <u>ah</u>-knees teh?
How old are you? (*informal*)	Quants anys tens?	kwans <u>ah</u>-knees tense?
I am .... years old	Jo tinc .... anys	joh teenk... <u>ah</u>-knees
Do you speak...?	Parles...?	<u>pahr</u>-lahs...
I (don't) speak...	Jo (no) parlo...	joh (noh) <u>pahr</u>-loo...
I speak a little... Catalan	Parlo una mica de... català	<u>pahr</u>-loo <u>oo</u>-nah <u>mee</u>-kah duh kah-tah-<u>lah</u>
Do you understand?	Comprens?	cohm-<u>prehns</u>
I (don't) understand	Jo (no) comprenc	joh (noh) cohm-<u>prehnk</u>
I (don't) know	Jo (no) sé	joh (noh) seh
I like it (very much)	M'agrada (molt)	mah-<u>grah</u>-dah (mol)
Where's the toilet, please?	El lavabo, si us plau?	ahl lah-<u>bah</u>-boo see yoos plow
I go to... school	Vaig a l'escola...	<u>bah</u>-itch ah lahs-<u>coh</u>-la...
Can you help me?	Pot ajudar-me?	pot ah-jew-<u>dahr</u> mah
I'm lost!	M'he perdut!	meh pahr-<u>doot</u>
Can you call my parents?	Pot trucar als meus pares?	pot troo-<u>kah</u> als <u>meh</u>-oos <u>pah</u>-ras
My parents' phone is...	El telèfon dels meus pares és...	ahl ta-<u>leh</u>-foon dahls <u>meh</u>-oos <u>pah</u>-ras ehss...

Numbers

ENGLISH	CATALAN	It sounds like...
1	Un	oon
2	dos	dohs
3	tres	trehs
4	quatre	kwah-trah
5	cinc	sink
6	sis	sees
7	set	seht
8	vuit	voo-eet
9	nou	noh-oo
10	deu	deh-oo
11	onze	ohn-zah
12	dotze	doh-tzah
13	tretze	treh-tzah
14	catorze	kah-thor-zah
15	quinze	keen-zah

ENGLISH	CATALAN	It sounds like...
16	setze	seh-tzah
17	diset	dee-seht
18	divuit	dee-voo-eet
19	dinou	dee-noh-oo
20	vint	veehnt
30	trenta	tren-tah
40	quaranta	kwuh-ran-tah
50	cinquanta	seen-kwahn-tah
60	seixanta	seh-ee-shan-tah
70	setanta	seh-tan-tah
80	vuitanta	voo-ee-tan-tah
90	noranta	noh-ran-tah
100	cent	sen
1000	mil	meel
0	zero	seh-roo

the juicy bits...

Damn, it's hot! (as in 'hot weather')	Keen ko-ee dah kah-lo
My brother is a pain	ahl meh-oo jar-mah es am-pra-nee-ah-door
My sister is a pain	lah meh-bah jar-mah-na es am-pra-nee-ah-door-ah
Bollocks!	keens koo-lee-ons
Damn!	rah-noh-ee
I don't give a rat's ass	mah lah soo-ah
You're a moron	ets oon sheem-plah [for him] ets oon-ah sheem-plah [for her]
You're hot	as-tahs boh [for him] / as-tahs boh-na [for her]

*For those 'older' readers: I know what you are thinking... but, c'mon guys I can't put it on a book!

Català | Español | English | Deutsch | Français | Euskara | Gallego | Occitan | 中文

intercat
Experience university in Catalan

HOME | I'M LEARNING CATALAN | SIGN ME UP! | LIVE IN CATALONIA | ACCESSIBILITY SITE MAP

Home / I'm learning Catalan / Resources for learning Catalan

I'm learning Catalan

Resources for learning Catalan
Conversation guides
Conversation guides App
Speakcat
TextOral
Gràcies Programme
Romànica Intercom
FortextCat
Arguments
Parla.cat
Paraules.cat
Class-Talk
The art of communication
20 writing tips

Catalan courses
Official Catalan certificates
Catalan abroad

Do you have any questions or suggestions?

Would you like to tell us about your experience?

Contact us

Did you know...

This region of universities have information on their e-community reply to the internet.

80 tips
On the Catalan characters

Lingoat
Information on the Catalan language

Experiences

Margarita do a language contact with it. Elena Varela enjoyed the experience and it enrols her to do full on the course website.

Language exchange

Do you want to learn Catalan?

Do you want to learn Catalan? We make it easy for you! With your effort and our help, you can do it. We provide you with a series of courses, guides and activities that will let you attain your goal.

In addition, we will tell you how you can obtain an official certificate in the Catalan language and will show you the resources that exist for you to stay in contact with Catalan from outside Catalonia.

There's no excuse. Speak Catalan!

Conversation guides

Level: Beginners
Aims: To help with first contact and to facilitate personal relations.
Skills: Comprehension of the language.
Mode of study: Online and paper format
further information

Speakcat

Level: Basic - Elementary
Aims: To discover the basic grammar and vocabulary of the Catalan language along with practical aspects of everyday university life.
Skills: Comprehension of the language.
Mode of study: Online
further information

TextOral

Level: Basic - Elementary
Skills: Oral and written comprehension
Mode of study: Classroom learning
further information

Gràcies Programme, Introduction to Catalan

Level: Basic
Skills: Oral and written comprehension
Mode of study: Classroom learning
further information

Romànica Intercom

Level: Acquisition of level A1 oral comprehension and between B1 and B2 written comprehension.
Aims: To develop independence in the reading of general texts in Portuguese, Spanish, Catalan, Italian and French in a very short time, between 30 and 40 hours, developing reading strategies that enable the rapid use of linguistic bridges between the different Romance languages.
Skills: Reading comprehension of five Romance languages.
Mode of study: Online
further information

20 writing tips

Level: Competence – advanced
Aims: To guarantee language quality and consistency in institutional and academic documents generated by universities.
Skills: Production of formal written texts appropriate to the university sphere.
Mode of study: Online
further information

El català amb tu
Catalan and you

Google play | App Store

The universities recommend

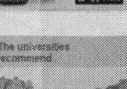

Have you got a language exchange partner? Would you like to go out with your partner and other UPF students?

Sortida a la Vall de Núria al Ripollès
Total activity: visit us from 1/6/2015
Sign up for our guided visits!

1 | 2 | 3

Do you know what this is?
Castell

A human tower of varying dimensions and structure, constituting a spectacular and moving act, in which men, women, girls and boys all cooperate to achieve a common feature.

Germany

What is Intercat? | Other websites | Legal note | Credits

Generalitat de Catalunya
Departament d'Economia i Coneixement

www.intercat.cat

PAGE 176

Biting into a piece of cake at Caelum...

Watching the sharks at l'Aquarium...
PAGE 26

Trolling around the city in a sightseeing tour bus, yes a tourist bus!...
PAGE 120

20 *things* I love to do in BARCELONA

Watching the street performers at La Rambla...

PAGE 42

Eating 'tapas' at La Llavor dels Origens...

PAGE 174

Visiting the Museu de la Ciència, a science museum where you can touch stuff...

PAGE 104

PAGE 44

Breathing history while strolling the Barri Gòtic, the old part of the city...

Catching a Barça football match at the Nou Camp...

PAGE 110

Riding the Sky Walk
attractions at El Tibidabo...

Visiting the monkeys
at the Zoo...

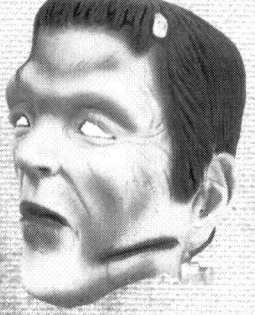

Buying
sweet treats
at La Boqueria...

Feeling the shivers down
my spine at the wax
museum...

Eating a delicious
crêpe at Annaick's...

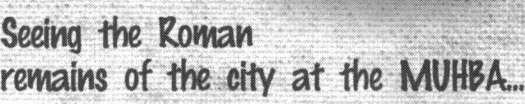

Seeing the Roman
remains of the city at the MUHBA...

(well, Port Aventura is not "in" the city, but it is only a train ride away).

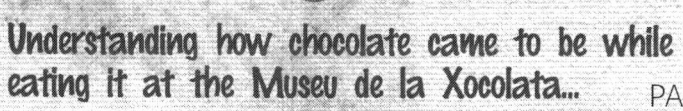

Useful **tips**

Knowing what's going on in the city...

CHECK THE CITY HALL'S WEBSITE AT WWW.BCN.CAT ● LIFESTYLE MAGA-
ZINES LIKE WWW.TIMEOUT.COM AND WWW.BARCELONA-METROPOLITAN.
COM ● OR THE GUIDE OUT, A FREE PAPER GUIDE AVAILABLE AT MANY
HOTEL INFORMATION DESKS AND RESTAURANTS ACROSS THE CITY

Foreign Consulates in Barcelona

Austria +34 934 537 294 ● Belgium +34 934 677 080 ● Brazil +34 934 882 288 ● Canada +34 932 703
614 ● China +34 932 541 199 ● Croatia +34 932 720 043 ● Czech Rep +34 932 413 236 ● Denmark
+34 934 875 486 ● Estonia +34 934 160 011 ● Finland +34 934 431 598 ● France +34 932 703 000 ●
Germany +34 932 921 000 ● Greece +34 933 212 828 ● Hungary +34 934 051 950 ● India +34 932
120 916 ● Ireland +34 934 915 021 ● Italy +34 902 050 141 ● India +34 932 120 916 ● Japan +34 932
803 433 ● Luxembourg +34 932 922 268 ● Mexico +34 932 011 822 ● Netherlands +34 934 199 580
● Norway +34 932 184 983 ● Poland +34 933 227 234 ● Portugal +34 933 188 150 ● Romania +34 934
181 535 ● Russian Federation +34 933 938 146 ● Slovakia +34 934 120 892 ● Slovenia +34 932 182
255 ● Sweden +34 934 882 501 ● Switzerland +34 934 090 650 ● Turkey +34 933 179 231 ● United
Kingdom +34 933 666 207 ● United States +34 932 802 227 ● Ukraine +34 932 804 009

Moving around

TRAIN

Rodalies de Catalunya (Tel. 900 410 041 local toll-free number, www.gencat.cat/rodalies), Ferrocarrils de la Generalitat-FGC (Tel. +34 932 051 515, www.fgc.cat). They operate different networks but they're interconnected, especially in and around Barcelona. For medium and long distance, RENFE (Tel. 902 320 320 local number, www.renfe.es).

Transfer to/from the airport

TAXI BARCELONA (Tel. +34 931 258 743, www.taxibarcelona.eu), RADIOTAXI BARCELONA (Tel. +34 932 933 111, www.radiotaxibarcelona.com). Note these two companies are guaranteed to have English-speaking staff. Others might or might not!

TAXI

Simply go into street and look for any passing black and yellow car. If the light on the roof is green, just raise your hand and it will stop. Note many drivers, especially the younger ones, do speak English... or at least they mumble it! A 10' ride in the city will cost you approximately 7 to 10.-€ -traffic permitting.

BUGGYING SERVICE

www.easytravelkids.com • www.babytravelling.com • www.lockerbarcelona.com

BABYSITTING (multilingual)

www.tlcanguros.com • www.bcnbabysitter.com • www.worldclassnannies.com

LUGGAGE STORAGE

Terminal 1 at Barcelona's airport • Sants train station • www.lockerbarcelona.com • www.citylockers.es • www.hastavuelo.com

NOTE REGARDING
• TAXI SERVICES •

All taxis legally operating in the city of Barcelona have to be painted black and yellow, any other colour and either it is not a city taxi –they can be from a different town- or it's not a taxi at all! Fares and services are regulated by the **Metropolitan Transport Institute** (IMT, www.taxibarcelona.cat) so no bartering or shady dealings are allowed. Fares must be always clearly visible when inside the taxi, normally in the form of a big sticker in the window. Always ask for a receipt. You can download a PDF with the current fares and services at the IMT website •

where to hire a...

BIKE, SEGWAY, SIDECAR, GO-CAR, SCOOTER, RICKSHAW, HELICOPTER

See activity # 46

Useful **tips**

Parks and gardens in the city

Most public parks open from 10am until 8 or 9pm (summer) and 6pm (winter)- albeit some are open spaces and they remain always open.

Zone: CENTRAL

• **Parc de la Ciutadella** (see #02) – Passeig Picasso, s/n – Metro: L4-Barceloneta, L1-Arc de Triomf – Recommended! • **Jardins Torre de les Aigües** – Roger de Llúria, 56 – Metro: L3-Passeig de Gràcia, L4-Girona • **Parc de l'Estació del Nord** – Nàpols, 70 – Metro: L1-Arc de Triomf, Tram: T4-Marina

Zone: WEST

• **Jardí Botànic (Botanical Gardens)** (see #30) – Dr. Font i Quer, 2 – Metro: L1-Espanya, L3-Espanya... then take the Funicular de Montjuïc – Recommended! • **Parc del Mirador del Migdia** – Passeig del Migdia, very close to Jardí Botànic – Metro: L1-Espanya, L3-Espanya... then take the Funicular de Montjuïc • **Parc Joan Miró** (known as "Parc de l'Escorxador") – Aragó, 2 – Metro: L1-Espanya, L3-Tarragona, L8-Espanya • **Parc de la Espanya Industrial** – Muntadas, 1 – Metro: L1-Plaça de Sants, L3-Sants • **Jardins Costa i Llobera** (a great cactus garden) – Carretera de Miramar – Metro: L2-Paralel, then a short walk... up hill – Recommended!

Zone: NORTH- WEST

• **Parc de Cervantes i Roserar** (see #43) (if you like roses!) – Avinguda Diagonal, 706 – Metro: L3-Zona Universitària – Recommended! • **Parc de Collserola** (see #44) – Carretera de l'Església, 92 – Bus: 118 and 128, S1-Baixador de Vallvidrera • **Parc del Castell de l'Oreneta** – Montevideo, 45 – Bus: 22 and 66 • **Jardins Eduard Marquina** (known as "Turó Park") – Avinguda de Pau Casals, 19 – Metro: L6-Muntaner • **Parc del Turó de Monterols** • Muntaner, 450 • Metro: L6-Muntaner • **Parc del Putxet** • Manacor, 29 – Metro: L3-Vallcarca – Recommended! • **Jardins de la Maternitat** – Travessera de les Corts, 159 – Metro: L3-Les Corts, Tram: T1-Pius XII • **Jardins de la Vil·la Santa Amèlia** – Santa Amèlia, 1 – Metro: L3-Maria Cristina, L6-Sarrià

Zone: EAST

• **Parc Central del Poble Nou** – Avinguda Diagonal, 130 – Tram: T4-Pere IV/Fluvià • **Parc Diagonal Mar** – Llull, 362 – Metro: L4-Selva de Mar, Tram: T4-Diagonal Mar • **Parc Infantil del Fòrum** – Plaça del Fòrum, 1 – Metro: L4-El Maresme-Forum, Tram: T4-Forum • **Parc de Sant Martí** – Menorca, 64 – Metro: L2-Sant Martí

Zone: NORTH-EAST

• **Parc Güell** (see #34) – Olot, 5 – Metro: L3-Vallcarca, then a short walk • Recommended! • **Parc de la Creueta del Coll** (see #35) – Passeig Mare de Déu del Coll, 77 – Metro: L5-El Coll/Teixonera • **Parc del Laberint (The Maze's Park)** (see #36) – Passeig dels Castanyers, 1 – Metro: L3-Llars Mundet – Recommended! • **Parc de les Aigües** – Abd El-Kader, s/n – Metro: L4-Alfons X

Non-dubbed cinemas
(uh-oh... mostly in English that is!)

• **Cine Yelmo - Icària** (see #28) – Centre de la Vil·la - Avinguda Icària, 154-166 – tel. +34 932 217 585 & 256 – www.yelmocines.es – Metro: L4-Ciutadella/Vila Olimpica – Recommended!

Zone: NORTH-EAST

• **Cinemes Verdi** – Verdi, 32 – tel. +34 932 387 990 – www.cines-verdi.com – Metro: L3-Fontana

Zone: NORTH-WEST

• **Cine Renoir–Les Corts** – Eugeni d'Ors, 12 – tel. +34 934 905 510 – www.cinesrenoir.com – Metro: L3-Les Corts

Zone: CENTRAL

• **Cinemes Melíes** – Vilarroel, 102 – tel. +34 934 510 051 – www.cinesmelies.net – Metro: L1-Urgell / L5-Hospital Clínic • **Cine Renoir– Floridablanca** – Floridablanca, 135 – tel. +34 934 263 337 – www.cinesrenoir.com – Metro: L2-Sant Antoni • **Cinemes Girona** – Girona, 175 – tel. +34 931 184 531 – www. cinemesgirona.cat – Metro: L4-Verdaguer, L5-Verdaguer • **Filmoteca de Catalunya** – Salvador Seguí, 1 – tel: +34 935 671 070 – Metro: L3-Liceu

ALSO...

Every summer, normally during July, Barcelona hosts **Sala Montjuïc**, an open-air film festival which presents concerts and films in a magnificent scenario: the Castell de Montjuïc (Montjuïc castle, overseeing Barcelona and the sea). You won't find the latest blockbusters in this festival, but a selection of the best movies of all times, including some for children. And please... feel free to bring your own snack and favourite drink along! All Sala Montjuïc films are screened in original version (non dubbed) with Spanish subtitles. It is recommendable to check the weather forecast a few days before the venue, especially if you want to buy the tickets in advance as the organisation does not refund them if it rains. You can find more information about Sala Montjuïc and the scheduled venues in their website (www.salamontjuic.org) •

The "Eixample"

The **Eixample** (pronounced 'eh-ee-sham-plah') is a district of Barcelona between the old city (Ciutat Vella) and what were once surrounding small towns (Sants, Gràcia, Sant Andreu...). It's characterized by long straight streets, a strict grid pattern crossed by wide avenues, and square blocks with chamfered corners. Due to this grid pattern, it's an extremely easy to navigate district •

AERIAL VIEW OF THE EIXAMPLE

Useful **tips**

Clubbing for teens

Have fun dancing to the latest hits

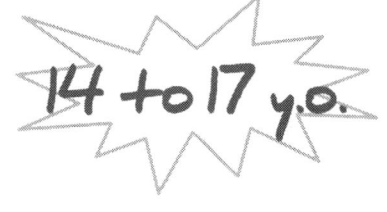

14 to 17 y.o.

If you are a die-hard music and dance lover, you're in luck, here in Barcelona you'll find a handful of clubs with so-called 'afternoon sessions' especially addressed (and only for!) teens aged 14-17. These sessions run normally on Saturday evenings, from 5pm to 10ish. You need to provide a valid ID proof to get in, whether it's your national ID card –if you have one in your country– or your passport. They're strictly alcohol free!

By the way, just for info, we differentiate between a 'club' and a 'discotheque' (or simply 'disco') and the verb *clubbing* is not really in our language. In fact, you'll hear people most often saying *"I'm going to the disco"*.

One of the most famous discos in town, **Up&Down**, has entertained Barcelona's youth since the 1960s. While it functions as a regular club for adults at nights, on Saturday it opens the doors to one of the coolest discos in town to teenagers, from 5pm to 9:30pm.

Other big hits are **Sweet Cherry** located in the 'poshest' area of Barcelona and **WOW Barcelona**, from the same business group.

A note for parents: it's OK to accompany your kid to the disco *-to the door, not inside, hey you don't wanna embarrass the kid!-* and pick him/her up at closing time. Many local parents do that, especially for the younger 'clubbers' •

Zone: NORTH-WEST

- **Up&Down** – Avinguda Doctor Marañon, 17, +34 934 486 115
- **Sweet cherry** – Carrer Beethoven, 18, +34 647 286 879

Zone: WEST

- **WOW Barcelona** – Carrer Tarragona, 141, +34 647 286 879

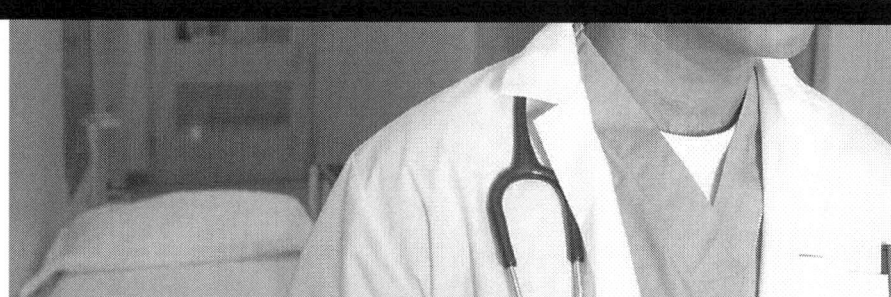

What to do if I get sick

Getting sick or having an accident while away from home can be alarming.

Be sure everyone brings all prescription medications, extra eyeglasses or contact lenses, health insurance information, and frequently used over-the-counter medication (such as for allergies, motion sickness, or upset stomach). Also, if you are a citizen of a European Union country, do not forget to bring your European Health Insurance Card (EHIC). Ask your parents.

Forgot your medication at home?, don't worry, over here you can buy most over-the-counter medication by going directly to any Farmàcia (pharmacy) and most major drug brands are available. If you're from outside the European Union you can even find that for some over-the-counter medication you don't even need a prescription from your doctor like you do when you're home. Boy, aren't we understanding over here!

But if you feel really sick, you can go to a local public health care centre –called CAPs (pronounced cahps), which stands for Centres for Primary Assistance- they are part of the state's public health network and there are several in each district of the city. Or if necessary, you can go to the A&E at any hospital for help. The nearer the better, isn't it? You can also call a doctor, day or night, to come to your place: dial the emergency number 112 and explain your problem to the operators. They will take care of everything and send a doctor –or an ambulance if needed- to your place. Note that not everybody speaks English... you can try using some of the sentences in Catalan provided in this book. If it's a busy shift it might take a while for the doctor to arrive, be patient.

There is good news though: in this country we have an excellent state-run health care system that in 2009 was ranked seventh best in the world by the World Health Organization. The system offers universal coverage to both locals and visitors and no out-of-pocket expenses -aside from prescription drugs. That means that your parents will probably have to pay next to nothing* for getting assistance! Super, eh?

Just in case, remember the words for 'I feel sick': "estic malalt" (pronounced ass-teak mah-lalt) in Catalan and "estoy enfermo" (pronounced es-toh-ee en-fehr-moh) in Spanish •

in case of EMERGENCY dial 112

Useful **tips**

Annual Festivals & Special Events

JANUARY
DIA DE REIS (THREE KINGS' DAY) • Jan 6th, gift giving festival with firework displays.
FESTES DELS TRES TOMBS • Jan 17th, part of the district festival of Sant Antoni Abat.

FEBRUARY
FEAST OF SANTA EULÀLIA • showcases of 'gegants' (giant papier maché heads) and medieval dances.

MARCH
CARNIVAL • this carnival is held at the beginning of Lenten season and there are also a series of religious festivals.

APRIL
FEAST OF SANT JORDI (ST GEORGE) • Apr 23rd, book stalls are set up and flowers are exchanged by couples.
FEAST OF VIRGIN OF MONTSERRAT • choir singing and 'sardana' dancing.

MAY
CORPUS CHRISTI • carpets of flowers and a 'dancing egg' is balanced on the Cathedral's fountain.
DIA DE SANT PONÇ • a herb fair in Carrer de l'Hospital, with flowers, cakes, sweets and aromatic oils.

CASTELLERS, DIA DE LA MERCÈ

JUNE
FEAST OF SANT JOAN • Jun 23rd to 24th with fireworks and general feasting.
GREC FESTIVAL • end June / beg. July, this is a festival of theatre, dance, music, circus and other stage arts.
SONAR • celebration of electronic music (Europe's biggest event of this kind).

JULY
SALA MONTJUÏC • lasting around six weeks. Open air cinema and concerts.

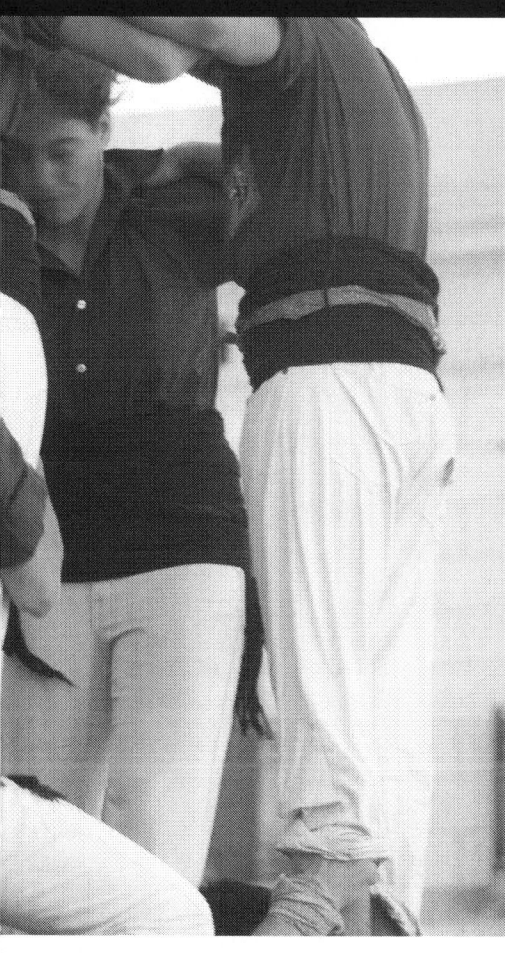

ELS CASTELLS

The "castells" (*pronunced kas-tehls*) are human towers built traditionally in festivals at many locations within Catalonia. At these festivals, several colles castelleres or teams often succeed in building and dismantling a tower's structure. This tradition originated in Valls, near the city of Tarragona, towards the end of the 18th century. In 2010, the castells were declared by UNESCO to be amongst the Masterpieces of the Oral and Intangible Heritage of Humanity •

BAM • around Sept 24th, free musical performances for the Festa de la Mercè, taking place in the squares, city centre and waterfront.

OCTOBER

FESTIVAL DE TARDOR • October to November, classical theatre, music, dance, cabaret and exhibitions.

NOVEMBER

FESTIVAL INTERNACIONAL DE JAZZ DE BARCELONA • lasting for about a week and many large venues in the city, this jazz festival features many jazz musicians.

AUGUST

ASSUMPTION FESTA MAJOR • Aug 15th to 21st, celebrations and local parties in the streets of Gràcia during the week leading up to Assumption.

SEPTEMBER

LA DIADA • Sept 11th Catalan national day with many demonstrations and much flag waving.
MARE DE DÉU DE LA MERCÈ (Our Lady of Mercy) • week of celebrations in honour of Barcelona's patron.

DECEMBER

CHRISTMAS FAIRS • many fairs and Christmas markets selling figurines and festive goods outside the cathedral and at the Sagrada Família.
SWIMMING CUP • Dec 25th, annual swimming cup where people dive into the icy waters of the port.
NEW YEAR'S EVE • general festivities and parties throughout Barcelona.

Solutions

to the Discovery Hunt

from page 188

1. **South west**, and more exactly, the spot where the ships were first sighted upon their return from the first trip to the Americas.

2. **Four**.

3. **Arts Santa Mònica** (pronounced: *arts sahn-tah moh-nee-ka*). You can visit many free art exhibitions there. Drop by if you like art and communication sciences.

5. **Seventy one** (15+23+15+18)

7. **Pla de La Boqueria**.

8. **Ajuntament** (City Hall) to the right and **Generalitat** to the left.

10. **L O P O V**, pronounced "*loh poh-oo*" which in old Catalan means 'the well' and it indicates that at that spot and underneath the street level there was a water well that served to supply drinking water to the citizens of the city.

12. **Four.** These are: the main entrance, the '*porta dels Sombrerers*' and '*porta de la Passioneria*' –also known as '*porta de les Moreres*'– at the sides, and '*porta del Born*' at the back. You've probably guessed by now that '*porta*' is Catalan for 'door'.

13. **CATALONIA**, which is the name of the region you're visiting now and whose capital is Barcelona. The term *Catalonia* originated around the 11th century in reference to the group of counties that comprised the *Marca Hispanica* set by the franks -rulers of what today is known as France. In 985, the Moorish army led by al-Mansur attacked Barcelona and the French king Hugh Capet did not honour a treaty by which he was bound to help the count of Barcelona to fight them back. After this treason, in 987 the count did not recognise the French king's dynasty anymore and put Catalonia effectively beyond Frankish rule, hence becoming an independent territory.

16. In **1876**.

17. **Estació de França** (or 'French Station' in English) and it's called like that because in the past the trains departing Barcelona for France left from this station, one of the four main stations in the city.

18. **Two**.

19. **La Ciutadella**.

20. The **Parliament of Catalonia**. It has 135 democratically elected members which represents the sovereignty of the people of Catalonia. The first documented meeting of the Catalan parliament was held in the year 1027!!!

22. **Four**. In the Roman period, a '*quadriga*' was a sort of car or chariot drawn by four horses abreast. In Latin, spoken by Romans, '*quadri-*' means 'four' and '*iugum*' means 'yoke'.

23. Four times three, equals **twelve steps**.

24. **Three**.

Metro**Network**   Lines&Stations

Alfons X **L4**
Almeda **L8**
Arc de Triomf **L1**
Artigues | Sant Adrià **L2**
Av. Tibidabo **L7**
Avinguda Carrilet **L1 L8**
Bac de Roda **L2**
Badal **L5**
Badalona P. Fabra **L2**
Barceloneta **L4**
Baró de Viver **L1**
Bellvitge **L1**
Besòs **L4**
Besòs Mar **L4**
Bogatell **L4**
Bon Pastor **L9 L10**
Camp de l'Arpa **L5**
Can Boixeres **L5**
Can Cuiàs **L11**
Can Peixauet **L9**
Can Serra **L1**
Can Vidalet **L5**
Can Zam **L9**
Canyelles **L3**
Casa de l'Aigua **L11**
Catalunya **L1 L3 L6 L7**
Ciutadella | V.Olimp. **L4**
Ciutat Meridiana **L11**
Clot **L1 L2**
Collblanc **L5**
Congrés **L5**
Cornellà Centre **L5**
Cornellà-Riera **L8**
Diagonal/Provença **L3 L5 L6 L7**
Drassanes **L3**
El Carmel **L5**
El Coll | la Teixonera **L5**
El Maresme | Fòrum **L4**
El Putxet **L7**
Encants **L2**
Entença **L5**
Església Major **L9**
Espanya **L1 L3 L8**
Europa | Fira **L8**
Fabra i Puig **L1**
Florida **L1**

Fondo **L1 L9**
Fontana **L3**
Gavarra **L5**
Girona **L4**
Glòries **L1**
Gorg **L2 L10**
Gornal **L8**
Gràcia **L6 L7**
Guinardó | Hosp. St. Pau **L4**
Horta **L5**
Hospital Clínic **L5**
Hospital de Bellvitge **L1**
Hostafrancs **L1**
Ildefons Cerdà **L8**
Jaume I **L4**
Joanic **L4**
La Bonanova **L6**
La Pau **L2 L4**
La Sagrera **L1 L5 L9 L10**
La Salut **L10**
Les Corts **L3**
Les Tres Torres **L6**
Lesseps **L3**
Liceu **L3**
Llacuna **L4**
Llefià **L10**
Llucmajor **L4**
Magòria - la Campana **L8**
Maragall **L4 L5**
Maria Cristina **L3**
Marina **L1**
Mercat Nou **L1**
Molí Nou | Ciutat Coop. **L8**
Montbau **L3**
Monumental **L2**
Mundet **L3**
Muntaner **L6**
Navas **L1**
Onze de Setembre **L9 L10**
Pàdua **L7**
Palau Reial **L3**
Paral·lel **L2 L3**
Passeig de Gràcia **L2 L3 L4**
Penitents **L3**
Pep Ventura **L2**
Pl. Molina **L7**

Plaça de Sants **L1 L5**
Plaça del Centre **L3**
Poble Sec **L3**
Poblenou **L4**
Pubilla Cases **L5**
Rbla. Just Oliveras **L1**
Reina Elisenda **L6**
Rocafort **L1**
Roquetes **L3**
Sagrada Família **L2 L5**
Sant Andreu **L1**
Sant Antoni **L2**
Sant Boi **L8**
Sant Gervasi **L6**
Sant Ildefons **L5**
Sant Josep **L8**
Sant Martí **L2**
St. Pau | Dos de Maig **L5**
Sant Roc **L2**
Santa Coloma **L1**
Santa Eulàlia **L1**
Santa Rosa **L9**
Sants-Estació **L3 L5**
Sarrià **L6**
Selva de Mar **L4**
Singuerlín **L9 L10**
Tarragona **L3**
Tetuan **L2**
Torras i Bages **L1**
Torrassa **L1**
Torre Baró | Vallbona **L11**
Trinitat Nova **L3 L4 L11**
Trinitat Vella **L1**
Universitat **L1 L2**
Urgell **L1**
Urquinaona **L1 L4**
Vall d'Hebron **L3 L5**
Vallcarca **L3**
Valldaura **L3**
Verdaguer **L4 L5**
Verneda **L2**
Via Júlia **L4**
Vilapicina **L5**
Virrei Amat **L5**
Zona Universitària **L3**

COLOR CODES

L1	RED	**L5**	BLUE	**L9**	ORANGE
L2	PURPLE	**L6**	LIGHT PURPLE	**L10**	LIGHT BLUE
L3	GREEN	**L7**	BROWN	**L11**	LIGHT GREEN
L4	YELLOW	**L8**	PINK		

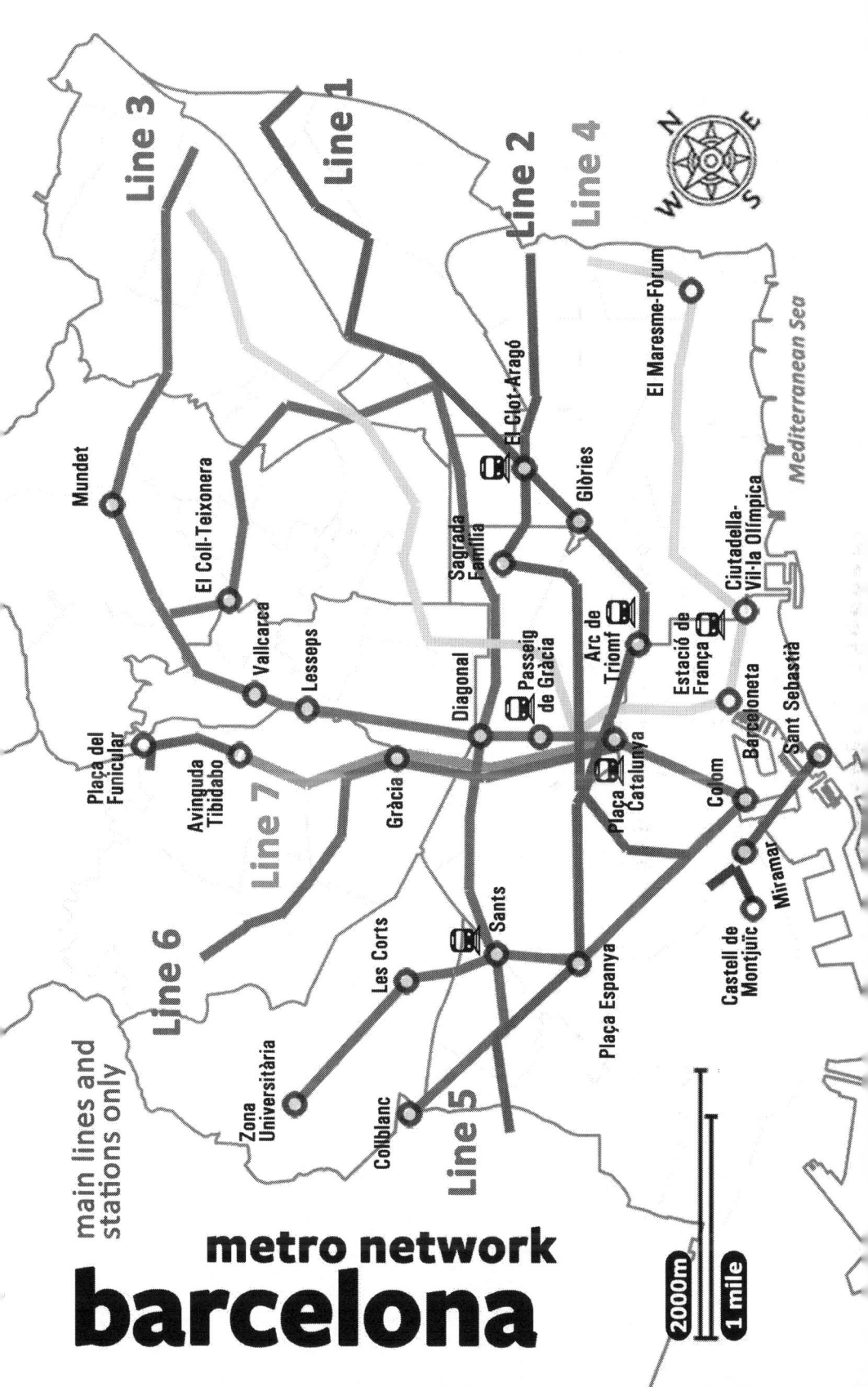

Index of
attractions&activities

Here's an index of all the places included in this guide arranged in alphabetical order

by zone in the city

SEE INDEX ON PAGE 17

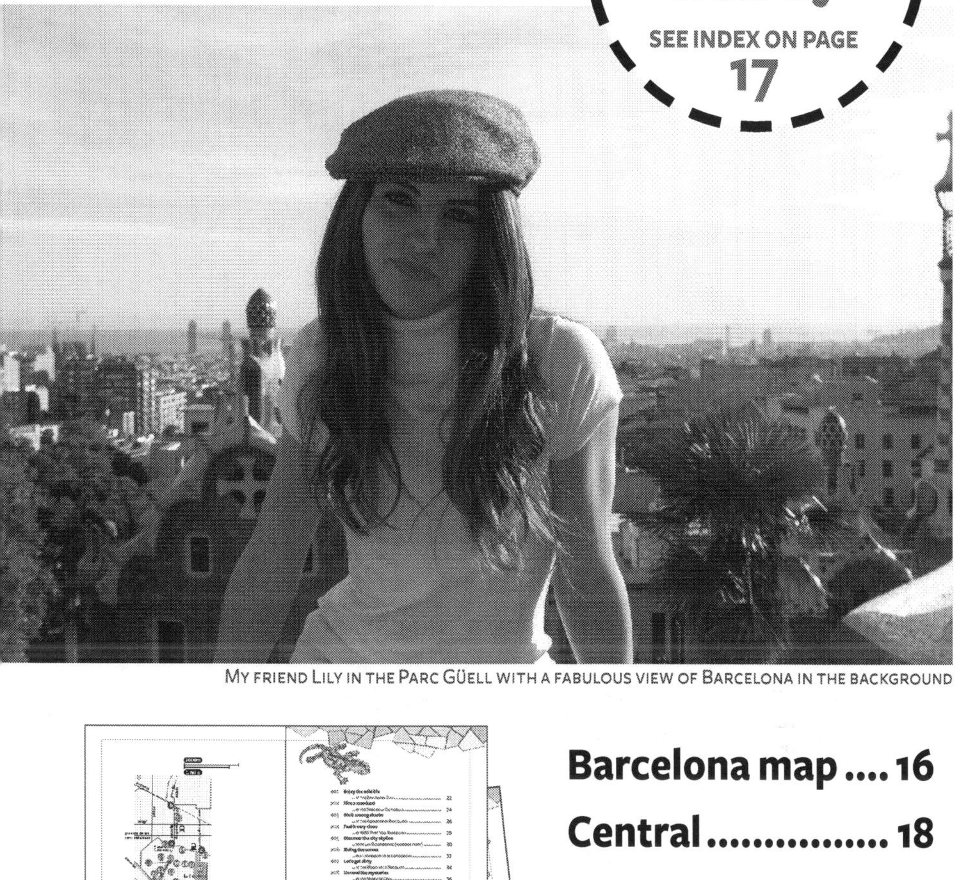

MY FRIEND LILY IN THE PARC GÜELL WITH A FABULOUS VIEW OF BARCELONA IN THE BACKGROUND

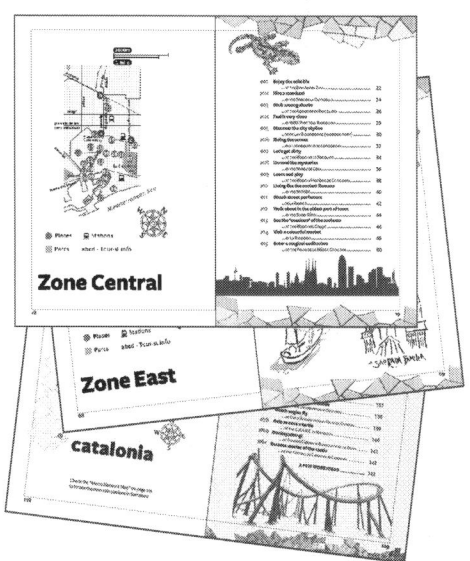

Indexbytype

Where
can
you...

...be active?

...do in a rainy day?

...make the most of a short stay?

...be 'not so' active?

...find animals?

...see sport?

...amusement parks?

General**index**

Your notes

Les teves notes

discovering
Barcelona
a travel guide for teens

thank you!

Author and design: ENRIC MASSÓ
Contact: enric@discoveringbarcelona.info
Contents updated as of: July 2013

An enormous debt of gratitude is owed to...

My nephews Laia and Pol and my sis Cristina who inspired me in the first place to write this guide. My cousin Gisel·la Massó and my friends Gigi Aspa, Ruben Maldonado, Catrina Bonet and Mike Stewart for their support and advice. Elena Lorente and Emma Casacuberta for their level-headed design talent and good humour. Drew Borrett and Manolo González for proof-reading and for their always spot-on suggestions. The wonderful mums Claire Brown, Audrey Wolf and Irina Gorbacheva for being my 'test subjects'. Emily Kerr and Joshua Perry who I have not met but I admire for their great guide "London Unlocked" that has shown me the way. A bunch of amateur Flickr photographers and my friends Lily Figuerola, Kelly Lodewyks and Mishka Moodly for letting me use their photos in this guide. My mum Helena for encouraging me. Ah yes, of course and to you for bothering to read these thankyous (and also for buying this book) •

Photo credits